What People Are Saying About Our Books

"Trusting a recipe often comes down to trusting the source.
The sources for the recipes are impeccable;
in fact, they're some of the best chefs in the nation."
BON APPETIT MAGAZINE

"Should be in the library—and kitchen—of every serious cook."
JIM WOOD—Food & Wine Editor—San Francisco Examiner

"A well-organized and user-friendly tribute to many of the state's
finest restaurant chefs."
SAN FRANCISCO CHRONICLE

"An attractive guide to the best restaurants and inns,
offering recipes from their delectable repertoire of menus."
GAIL RUDDER KENT—Country Inns Magazine

"Outstanding cookbook"
HERITAGE NEWSPAPERS

"I couldn't decide whether to reach for my telephone and make reservations
or reach for my apron and start cooking."
JAMES MCNAIR—Best-selling cookbook author

"It's an answer to what to eat, where to eat—and how to do it yourself."
THE MONTEREY HERALD

"I dare you to browse through these recipes
without being tempted to rush to the kitchen."
PAT GRIFFITH—Chief, Washington Bureau, Blade Communications, Inc.

Books of the "Secrets" Series

COOKING SECRETS

GUIDEBOOK & COOKBOOK

AMERICA'S SOUTH

Kathleen DeVanna Fish

BON
VIVANT

Library of Congress Cataloging-in-Publication Data

Cooking Secrets of America's South
The Chefs' Secret Recipes
Fish, Kathleen DeVanna
97-071563
ISBN 1-883214-11-4
$15.95 softcover
Includes indexes
Autobiography page

Copyright ©1997 by Kathleen DeVanna Fish
Cover photograph by Robert N. Fish
Editorial direction by Judie Marks
Editorial assistance by Nadine Guarrera
Cover design by Morris Design
Illustrations by Krishna Gopa, Graphic Design and Illustration
Type by Cimarron Design

Published by Bon Vivant Press
a division of The Millennium Publishing Group
P.O. Box 1994
Monterey, CA 93942

Printed in the United States of America
by Publishers Press

Contents

Prepare to Be Tempted…

Cooking Secrets from America's South captures the flavors and spirit of the South. It offers you inside information on the best restaurants and inns—and it reveals the secret recipes of 66 of the region's greatest chefs. You probably will recognize some of the cooking stars. And you will meet a new galaxy of master chefs. None of the chefs paid to be included in this book. They—and their restaurants and inns—were hand-selected and invited to participate. The requirements: excellence of food, consistency of quality and a flair for beautiful presentation.

The very selective list of restaurants includes some that are elegant, some that are comfortably casual and some that the locals would prefer to keep secret. The determining factor is fabulous food.

We also include recommendations for unforgettable places to stay. Each inn was chosen because it is so enchanting, so perfect in service and ambience that you will luxuriate in the surroundings. Drawings of each inn by our artist will help you decide where to stay.

We took the chefs' recipes—165 of them—and adapted them for the home cook. Some of the recipes are simple. Some are more complex. We stayed clear of purely trendy food, preferring to stress dishes that we know are wonderful. To make your life easier, we include preparation times and cooking times. And we list the recipes in these handy categories: Breakfast, Appetizers, Soups, Salads and Dressings, Seafood, Poultry, Game, Meats, Main Courses, Pasta and Grains, Vegetables and Side Dishes and Final Temptations.

The 165 kitchen-tested recipes feature such enticing dishes as Creole Crab Cakes with Pico de Gallo, Crawfish and Mushroom Gumbo, Goat Cheese and Arugula Salad with Lavender-Vanilla Vinaigrette, Shrimp Creole, Grilled Pork Chops with Green Tomato Relish, Spicy Shrimp, Sausage and Tasso Gravy over Creamy White Grits and Maple Pecan Tart with Chocolate Sorbet.

Prepare to be tempted.

Southern Restaurants and Inns

Alabama

Georgia

Louisiana

Mississippi

North Carolina

South Carolina

Tennessee

Chefs' Favorite Recipes

Breakfast and Breads

Southern Biscuits—**Richmond Hill Inn**, *225*

Italian Cracked Wheat Bread—**Buckhorn Inn**, *273*

Cornbread—**The Pirate's House**, *94*

French Toast—**Fleur de Lis Bed and Breakfast**, *155*

Southern Frittata—**1790 House Bed and Breakfast**, *249*

Asparagus and Ham Mornay—**Arrowhead Inn**, *215*

Bran Muffins—**Millsaps Buie House**, *185*

Carrot, Zucchini and Apple Muffins—**John Rutledge House Inn**, *251*

Fresh Cherry Muffins—**Le Jardin Sur Le Bayou**, *163*

Tropical Muffins—**Forsyth Park Inn**, *99*

Cranberry-Raisin Scones—**Greyfield Inn**, *101*

Appetizers

Baked Brie en Croute with Brown Sugar and Almonds—
Jekyll Island Club Hotel, *103*

Shrimp and Crab Meat Cheesecake—**Broussard's**, *125*

Duck Confit with Hummus, Spiced Tomato and Phyllo—**Collector's Café**, *237*

Duck Confit, Apple and Cranberry Compote—
The Fairview at the Washington Duke Inn and Golf Club, *203*

Crab Cakes—**Loews Vanderbilt Plaza Hotel**, *275*

McCellenville Crabcakes—**82 Queen**, *233*

Creole Crab Cakes with Pico de Gallo—**Bella Luna**, *119*

Marinated Crab Fingers—**Joe's "Dreyfus Store" Restaurant**, *133*

Crab Meat Maison—**Galatoire's**, *129*

Pan-Fried Soft-Shell Crab with Lobster Slaw and Yellow Tomato Vinaigrette—**City Grill**, *71*

Pan-Fried Soft-Shell Crab with a Shrimp and Crab Meat Butter Cream Sauce—**Nick's**, *179*

Hot Artichoke Dip—**Loyd Hall Plantation**, *165*

Morel Mushroom Blue Cheese Gratin—**The Market Place**, *207*

Pan-Fried Chicken Livers, Caramelized Onions and Ham, Red-Eye Gravy—**Magnolias Uptown/Down South**, *244*

Grilled Portobello Mushroom Topped with Tarragon Accented Vegetables—**1587**, *195*

Sautéed Shiitake and Portobello Mushrooms with Goat Cheese—**Pillars**, *35*

Oyster Six Shot—**Palace Café**, *141*

Oysters Bienville—**Arnaud's**, *111*

Oysters en Brochette—**Galatoire's**, *130*

Oysters, Spinach, Goat Cheese Beggars Purse, Apple-Smoked Bacon Vinaigrette—**Hotel Maison de Ville**, *157*

Grilled Gulf Shrimp with Corn and Lima Bean Ragout and Louisiana Hot Sauce Beurre Blanc—**Liza's**, *173*

Mushroom-Couscous Strudel—**212 Market**, *263*

Oyster Sausage Turnover with Apple Horseradish Sauce—**Elizabeth on 37th**, *79*

Soups

Beet Soup with Sour Cream and Apple Smoked Bacon—**The Market Place**, *208*

Bouillabaisse with Herb Croutons and Rouille Sauce—**Palace Café**, *142*

Broccoli Soup—**Prudhomme's Cajun Café**, *151*

Corn and Shrimp Soup—**Joe's "Dreyfus Store" Restaurant**, *134*

Charleston She Crab Soup—**82 Queen**, *234*

Garlic, Broccoli and White Bean Soup—**Aurora**, *200*

Gumbo Ya Ya—**Lyric Springs Country Inn**, *277*

Crawfish and Mushroom Gumbo—**Hotel Maison de Ville**, *158*

Okra Gumbo—**The Pirate's House**, *91*

Louisiana Seafood Gumbo—**Lafitte's Landing**, *137*

Shrimp Gumbo—**The Rhett House Inn**, *255*

Winter Leek and Potato Soup—**Meadowlark Farm**, *30*

Wild Mushroom Soup with Lobster and White Port—**Collector's Café**, *239*

Trio of Wild Mushrooms and Smoked Duckling Soup—**Prejean's**, *147*

New Zealand Mussels in a Mediterranean Chardonnay Broth—**1587**, *196*

Peach Soup—**The Cloister**, *97*

Golden Pear Soup—**Meadowlark Farm**, *29*

Southern Velvet Soup—**Opryland Hotel**, *281*

Butternut Squash Soup with Roasted Pumpkin Seed Oil—**Bacchanalia**, *57*

Turtle Soup au Sherry—**Voyagers**, *43*

Salads and Dressings

Caprino Salad—**Aurora**, *199*

Warm Roasted Corn and Black Bean Salad—**Pine Needles Lodge and Golf Club**, *223*

Greens with Tarragon Dressing and Seasoned Almonds—**La Tourelle**, *265*

Goat Cheese and Arugula Salad with Lavender Vanilla Vinaigrette—
Pewter Rose, *211*

Honey and Herb Dressing over Baby Greens—**Meadowlark Farm**, *31*

Hearts of Palm Salad—**Pillars**, *36*

Seafood

Sautéed Shrimp En Pesto—**Voyagers**, *44*

Baked Snapper with Grilled Pineapple—**Bella Luna**, *121*

Swordfish with Wild Mushroom Hash—**Aurora**, *201*

Trout Meunière Amandine—**Galatoire's**, *131*

Roasted Trout with Pancetta and Olive Tapenade—**Union Station Hotel**, *283*

Poultry

Ancho Pepper Honey-Glazed Chicken Breast with Corn and Black Bean Relish—
Richmond Hill Inn, *226*

Grilled Chicken with Tomato and Basil Sauce—**Meadowlark Farm**, *32*

Chicken and Dumplings—**Mrs. Wilkes' Boarding House**, *87*

Roast Duck Breast, Wild Mushroom Stuffing and Sun-Dried Cherry Sauce—
Pine Needles Lodge and Golf Club, *221*

Game

*Apple Smoked Bacon Wrapped Quail Breasts with Sage Risotto Cakes in a Warm Mustard
Pecan Vinaigrette*—**Southside Grill**, *269*

Grilled Quail with Spicy Creamed Collard Greens—**Bacchanalia**, *58*

Quail with Plum Sauce—**Monmouth Plantation**, *187*

Crescent City Quail—**Prejean's**, *149*

Jamaican Jerk Grilled Cervena Venison, Tropical Vegetable Sauté—**1587**, *197*

Meat

Filet Mignon—**Voyagers**, *45*

Roasted Double Lamb Chops with Fresh Herbs and Vegetables—**Vintage Year**, *40*

Lamb Roast or Rack with Garden Herbs—**Meadowlark Farm**, *33*

Main Courses

Pasta and Grains

Vegetables and Side Dishes

Final Temptations

Cooking Stars of America's South

82 QUEEN

CHARLESTON, SOUTH CAROLINA
(803) 723-7591
Page 232

212 MARKET

CHATTANOOGA, TENNESSEE
(423) 265-1212
Page 262

1587

ROANOKE ISLAND, NORTH CAROLINA
(919) 473-1587
Page 194

ARNAUD'S

NEW ORLEANS, LOUISIANA
(504) 523-5433
Page 110

AURORA

CHAPEL HILL, NORTH CAROLINA
(919) 942-2400
Page 198

BACCHANALIA

ATLANTA, GEORGIA
(404) 365-0410
Page 56

BELLA LUNA

NEW ORLEANS, LOUISIANA
(504) 529-583
Page 118

BONE'S

ATLANTA, GEORGIA
(404) 237-2663
Page 62

BROUSSARD'S

NEW ORLEANS, LOUISIANA
(504) 581-3866
Page 124

BUCKHEAD DINER

ATLANTA, GEORGIA
(404) 262-3336
Page 66

CITY GRILL
ATLANTA, GEORGIA
(404) 524-2489
Page 70

COLLECTOR'S CAFÉ
MYRTLE BEACH, SOUTH CAROLINA
(803) 449-9370
Page 236

ELIZABETH ON 37TH
SAVANNAH, GEORGIA
(912) 236-5547
Page 78

THE FAIRVIEW AT THE WASHINGTON DUKE INN AND GOLF CLUB
DURHAM, NORTH CAROLINA
(919) 490-0999
Page 202

GALATOIRE'S
NEW ORLEANS, LOUISIANA
(504) 525-2021
Page 128

IL PASTICCIO

SAVANNAH, GEORGIA

(912) 231-8888

Page 84

JOE'S "DREYFUS STORE" RESTAURANT

LIVONIA, LOUISIANA

(504) 637-2625

Page 132

LAFITTE'S LANDING

ST. JAMES, LOUISIANA

(504) 473-1232

Page 136

LA TOURELLE

MEMPHIS, TENNESSEE

(901) 726-5771

Page 264

LIZA'S

NATCHEZ, MISSISSIPPI

(601) 446-6368

Page 172

MAGNOLIAS UPTOWN/DOWN SOUTH

CHARLESTON, SOUTH CAROLINA

(803) 577-7771

Page 242

THE MARKET PLACE

ASHEVILLE, NORTH CAROLINA

(704) 252-4162

Page 206

MEADOWLARK FARM

ALABASTER, ALABAMA

(205) 663-3141

Page 28

MRS. WILKES' BOARDING HOUSE

SAVANNAH, GEORGIA

(912) 232-5997

Page 86

NICK'S

JACKSON, MISSISSIPPI

(601) 981-8017

Page 178

PALACE CAFÉ

NEW ORLEANS, LOUISIANA

(504) 523-1661

Page 140

THE PALETTE RESTAURANT AT THE MISSISSIPPI MUSEUM OF ART

JACKSON, MISSISSIPPI

(601) 960-1515

Page 182

PEWTER ROSE

CHARLOTTE, NORTH CAROLINA

(704) 332-8149

Page 210

PILLARS

MOBILE, ALABAMA

(334) 478-6341

Page 34

THE PIRATE'S HOUSE

SAVANNAH, GEORGIA

(912) 233-5757

Page 90

ALABAMA:
The Heart Of Dixie

Cherokee, Chickasaw, Choctaw and Creek Indians—long time inhabitants of what is today's Alabama—were none too pleased when the Spanish explorer Hernando de Soto first led an expedition to the Gulf Coast in 1540. During the next two centuries, the French, British and Spanish struggled for control of the area. It was not until 1702 that the French established Alabama's first permanent settlement at Mobile.

Despite the natural softness of the land—coastal plain giving way to broken hills, with rich black marl soil and ample minerals, with long, hot summers, mild winters and abundant rainfall—Alabama has witnessed the harsh footsteps of men determined to make it their own. Future President Andrew Jackson defeated the Creek Confederacy in 1814, ending Native American resistance in the South and paving the way for Alabama's entry into the Union as the 22nd state in 1819. The development of the cotton gin and the emergence of King Cotton drove the Indians farther west, beyond Alabama's borders.

Another Confederacy—that of the American South—was born in Montgomery, when, in 1861, the Ordinance of Secession was passed in that city. Jefferson Davis became the President of the Confederate States of America and his "little White House" was established there.

After the Civil War, Alabama witnessed the timeless grace of Helen Keller and, in 1915, the devastation of the cotton industry by the notorious boll weevil. Faced with economic oblivion, the state reacted with a vengeance. Agriculture diversified, as King Cotton, now *Rex Emeritus,* was dethroned by peanuts and soybeans. Defense industries boosted the urban economy in World War II, and after the war, Alabama witnessed the birth of the American Space Program, with the development of NASA's Marshall Space Flight Center at Huntsville.

Alabama is home to Americans as diverse as sports figures Hank Aaron, Bo Jackson, Joe Louis, Willie Mays and Jesse Owens; actress Tallulah Bankhead; Hugo L. Black, a former member of the Ku Klux Klan, who became one of the great liberal Justices of the United States Supreme Court; entertainers Nat "King" Cole, W.C. Handy and Hank Williams; and scientists George Washington Carver and Booker T. Washington. The legacy of one time Governor George Wallace may be gone and forgotten. But the state's motto, "We dare defend our rights," tempered by warm Southern hospitality and the ethereal mists that still haunt Alabama's ante-bellum mansions, make it an inviting, exciting destination.

Here are some of the highlights of a trip to Alabama.

BIRMINGHAM: Alabama's largest city was nothing more than empty farmland and a steel boomtown when it was founded in 1871. Today's Birmingham, with more than a quarter-million people, is strikingly different from what it was only twenty years ago. Pollution-spewing steel and manufacturing smokestacks are gone, replaced by a renovated central business district and a smog-free skyline. When visiting, you are sure to enjoy the ARLINGTON ANTEBELLUM HOME AND GARDENS, a fine example of Greek revival architecture dating from the 1840s and furnished in pre-Civil War style; the BIRMINGHAM BOTANICAL GARDENS, nearly seventy acres of flowers, trees and shrubs with a conservatory housing more than 5,000 species of plants and 230 species of birds; and the BIRMINGHAM CIVIL RIGHTS INSTITUTE.

Birmingham's Civil Rights Institute.

*Photo: Dan Brothers,
Alabama Bureau of Tourism and Travel*

THE AVE MARIA GROTTO AT CULLMAN, on the grounds of the St. Bernard Abbey. Over a period of more than fifty years, Brother Joseph, using pictures as a guide, decorated the main grotto with dioramas depicting Biblical events and created more than 120 miniatures of famous churches, buildings and shrines from many parts of the world. Construction materials range from bits of discarded glass and jewelry to native stone and marble. Since the grotto is situated in an old quarry, the landscape is accentuated by gently sloping paths.

EUFALA. Ante-bellum homes done in Greek Revival, Italianate and Victorian 19th century homes are the hallmark of this former stronghold of the Creek Confederacy, now a charming haven off the beaten track of the new century.

You should not miss the **UNITED STATES ARMY AVIATION MUSEUM** at Fort Rucker. There are many one-of-a-kind planes, including the first military production helicopter, the most recent military attack helicopter, and a collection of World War I aircraft.

HUNTSVILLE, considered the birthplace of the nation's space program, is home to the Saturn V moon rocket designed here by Dr. Wernher von Braun. The United States Space and Rocket Center features one of the world's largest collections of space and rocket hardware and a simulation of travel aboard a space shuttle. The TWICKENHAM HISTORIC DISTRICT is one of Alabama's largest ante-bellum residential districts. Descendants of the original owners still live in many of the homes. The district is a living museum of 19th century architecture.

MOBILE'S MARDI GRAS, though smaller in size than the celebration in New Orleans, is the original American pre-Lenten carnival. First observed in 1703 and suspended during the Civil War, the festivities were revived in 1866. The merrymaking begins during Thanksgiving, with a ball each week until Ash Wednesday. During the two weeks before Lent, a different mystic society parades each evening. While in Mobile, you'll pinch yourself if you don't visit the USS ALABAMA BATTLESHIP MEMORIAL, a 100-acre park dedicated to veterans who served during World War II, the Korean War, the Vietnam War and Desert Storm. The centerpieces of the memorial are the battleship USS *Alabama,* the World War II submarine USS *Drum,* a B-52 bomber, World War II fighter planes, the A-12 Blackbird spy plane and a captured Iraqi tank.

Historic **MONTGOMERY** will have you turning your head to see its hundred facets, from the nationally famous ALABAMA SHAKESPEARE FESTIVAL to the FIRST WHITE HOUSE OF THE CONFEDERACY, to OLD ALABAMA TOWN. But perhaps the most unique place in this city is the F. SCOTT AND ZELDA FITZGERALD MUSEUM—situated in the house the Fitzgeralds occupied during his writing of *Tender Is The Night* and her writing of *Save Me The Waltz*. Zelda was born in Montgomery.

A re-enactment of the Civil War Battle of Selma, Alabama

Photo: Dan Brothers, Alabama Bureau of Tourism and Travel

SYLACAUGA is built on a foundation of solid white marble, which has been used since the 1840's to construct notable buildings throughout the country, including the U.S. Supreme Court building in Washington, DC.

TUSCUMBIA is home to the Helen Keller Birthplace and Shrine. Deaf and blind from the age of 18 months, the indomitable Miss Keller not only succeeded in learning the things that unimpaired children learn, but also graduated cum laude from Radcliffe College in 1904. She gained worldwide recognition for her work on behalf of deaf and blind people and women's rights. Her home at Ivy Green contains many of its original furnishings, a library of Braille books, a Braille typewriter and gifts from 25 countries.

The **GEORGE WASHINGTON CARVER MUSEUM** at Tuskegee follows this great African-American's careers as an artist, teacher and scientist. His preserved laboratory displays the results of his experiments with farm and forest products. Part of the Tuskegee Institute National Historical Site.

☆

MEADOWLARK FARM

Meadowlark Farm
EUROPEAN CUISINE
534 Industrial Road
Alabaster, Alabama
(205) 663-3141
Dinner Wednesday–Saturday 5:30PM–10:30PM
AVERAGE DINNER FOR TWO: $70

 t the end of a winding driveway you will find Meadowlark Farm, a charming house located in the hinterlands of Shelby County. Here the menu changes at the chef's whim, reflecting the freshest foods of the season.

Dining tables are scattered throughout the restaurant with settings of fine china and silver, candles and fresh flowers. Soft lighting enhances the Renaissance prints and framed scarves that adorn the walls.

The wine list includes selections from California, France, Germany and Australia. Menu highlights include Grilled Duck Breast served with Duchess Potatoes, Braised Red Cabbage and Acorn Squash. The Gulf Snapper is stuffed with seasoned vegetables and accompanied with a Sweet Vidalia Onion Chutney. Save room for the Chocolate Symphony, which is a delightful variation of Creme Brûlée.

MEADOWLARK FARM'S MENU FOR SIX

Golden Pear Soup

Leek and Potato Soup

Honey and Herb Dressing over Baby Greens

Grilled Chicken with Tomato and Basil Sauce

Lamb Roast or Rack with Garden Herbs

Golden Pear Soup

C ook yams in chicken broth with cinnamon stick. Peel and core the pears, then cut in slices and sauté with butter until soft. Add the wine.

Purée the pears and yams slowly, adding the broth from the yams. Add the cream or sour cream until soup is a velvety-textured consistency. Season with salt and pepper to taste.

Serve warm and garnish with nutmeg.

Serves 10
Preparation Time:
  One Hour

1½ lbs. yams
 4 cups chicken broth
 1 cinnamon stick
 4 large ripe pears (do not use Bosc pears)
 2 Tbsps. butter
 ¼ cup white wine
 ½ cup cream or sour cream
   Salt and pepper to taste
   Nutmeg, garnish

Winter Leek and Potato Soup

Serves 6
Preparation Time:
One Hour

½ stick butter
1 lb. potatoes, peeled, sliced
1 onion, peeled, sliced
1 lb. leeks, sliced
3 cups chicken stock
  Salt and pepper to taste
1 cup half and half, or to taste
½ cup milk
1 Tbsp. bacon drippings
  Sour cream, garnish
  Parsley or chives, garnish

Melt the butter in a saucepan; when it foams, add the potatoes, onion and leeks, coat with butter. Sweat on gentle heat until the vegetables are soft. Add the stock and boil until the vegetables are cooked.

Purée and season to taste.

Add the cream, milk and bacon drippings.

Serve with a dollop of sour cream and chopped parsley or chives.

☆

Honey and Herb Dressing over Baby Greens

Place all the dressing ingredients in a blender or shaker, add the salt and pepper to taste. Blend for a few seconds.

Pour dressing over baby greens. Toss well.

Cooking Secret: Garnish with tomatoes, mushrooms, bacon bits or nuts.

As a variation, you can use fresh lemon juice or wine vinegar instead of cider vinegar.

Serves 6
Preparation Time:
 5 Minutes

¾ cup virgin olive oil
4 Tbsps. cider vinegar
1 tsp. honey
1 garlic clove, minced
2 Tbsps. fresh herbs, chopped (parsley, chives, mint, watercress, basil, thyme, etc.)
 Salt and pepper to taste
1 lb. baby salad greens

Grilled Chicken with Tomato and Basil Sauce

Serves 6
Preparation Time:
  1¼ Hours
Preheat oven to 350°

  12 **Tbsps. butter**
      (1½ sticks)
   6 **chicken breasts**
      Salt and pepper to
      taste
   1 **cup cream**
   4 **tomatoes, ripe yet firm**
      Sugar to taste, optional
  15 **basil leaves**

Heat a sauté pan very hot. Place 4 Tbsps. butter on chicken breasts and season with salt and pepper. Sauté the breasts until golden brown, turning on both sides.

Remove from stove top and place in a 350° oven for 8 to 12 minutes, checking with a knife for any pink sections. The chicken should be moist and juicy, but cooked through.

Pour the cream into a saucepan and heat until it thickens and is on the edge of burning. Whisk in 8 Tbsps. (1 stick) butter in cubes, until a creamy sauce results.

Peel the tomatoes, quarter and remove seeds. Cut the tomato into ½-inch cubes and season with the salt, pepper and sugar. Mix this into the sauce with the chopped basil leaves. Cut the basil just before mixing. Reheat sauce gently just before serving.

To serve, spoon the tomato and basil sauce on a plate; slice the breast of chicken and fan slightly in the center of sauce.

Cooking Secret: The sugar is to just take the acid edge off the tomato, so be careful.

Lamb Roast or Rack with Garden Herbs

T o make the herb relish, place 1 cup herbs, olive oil and garlic cloves in blender for a minute or so until a green paste is formed.

Trim the lamb, rub and coat with the herb relish. Coat the rack with some bread crumbs; it protects the herbs while cooking. Let marinade for an hour or so.

Roast in oven at 350° for 1¼ hours for rare; 1½ hours for medium; or 1¾ hours for well done. A rack of lamb, being smaller, will roast for 30 to 45 minutes. It will have to be checked with a meat thermometer.

Degrease the juices in a roasting pan, add the stock and bring to a boil.

Blend the flour in a small heavy saucepan with enough butter to make a loose paste or roux. Add the roux to the stock for a thicker sauce if desired.

Serves 8 to 10
  (Rack Serves 2)
Preparation Time:
  1 Hour
(note marinating time)
Preheat oven to 350°

  1 leg of lamb (about 7 to
     8 pounds) or 1 lamb
     rack
  1 cup + 2 tsps. puréed
     herbs (basil, parsley,
     thyme, lemon balm,
     mint, tarragon, chives,
     rosemary & marjoram)
  1 cup olive oil
  3 large garlic cloves
     Salt and pepper to
     taste
2½ cups lamb or chicken
     stock
  ⅓ cup flour
  4 Tbsps. butter

PILLARS

Pillars
CONTINENTAL CUISINE
1757 Government Street
Mobile, Alabama
(334) 478-6341
Dinner Monday–Saturday 5PM–10PM
AVERAGE DINNER FOR TWO: $60

Mobile Bay has enticed Europeans from the earliest days of exploration. Its historic Southern charm still lures travelers from near and far.

That charm called to Filippo Milone, a Sicilian chef trained in Europe, who made Mobile his home and opened Pillars in 1976, restoring a historical white-column house to its turn-of-the-century Neoclassical grandeur. Furnished with antiques, the restaurant conjures up an intimate atmosphere despite its size—there are 11 dining rooms—and serves up its fine cuisine in ultra-romantic surroundings.

In addition to an extensive menu, Pillars offers four nightly fixed-price "Epicurean Dinners."

Some of the menu highlights include Shrimp Cocktails, Fresh Mozzarella Salad, Veal Scaloppini al Marsala, Ziti with Sautéed Mushrooms and Smoked Duck Sausage, Amaretto Cheesecake and Caramel Custard. The breads, sauces and vegetables are all homemade.

PILLAR'S MENU FOR SIX

Sautéed Shiitake and Portobello Mushrooms with Goat Cheese

Hearts of Palm Salad

Veal Scaloppini Bologna Style

Sautéed Shiitake and Portobello Mushrooms with Goat Cheese

I n a large sauté pan melt the butter and olive oil over medium heat. Add the mushrooms and sauté until cooked through.

In a mixing bowl, combine the goat cheese, thyme and extra-virgin olive oil and mix until well blended. Season to taste.

Divide the hot mushrooms on individual serving plates and top each serving with the cheese mixture.

Serves 6
Preparation Time:
  15 Minutes

2 Tbsps. butter
2 Tbsps. olive oil
1 lb. shiitake
  mushrooms, cleaned,
  sliced
1 lb. portobello
  mushrooms, cleaned,
  sliced
1 cup goat cheese
1 tsp. thyme
3 Tbsps. extra-virgin
  olive oil
  Salt and pepper to
  taste

★

Hearts of Palm Salad

Serves 6
Preparation Time:
15 Minutes

1 lb. baby lettuce leaves
12 hearts of palm stalks,
cut in half lengthwise
12 tomato slices
6 hard boiled eggs, cut
into quarters
2 Tbsps. balsamic
vinegar
4 Tbsps. extra-virgin
olive oil
Salt and pepper to
taste
Fresh parsley, chopped

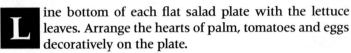 ine bottom of each flat salad plate with the lettuce leaves. Arrange the hearts of palm, tomatoes and eggs decoratively on the plate.

Drizzle the top with balsamic vinegar and olive oil. Season with salt and pepper to taste. Garnish with fresh parsley.

☆

Veal Scaloppini Bologna Style

L ightly pound the veal slices to flatten and dip them into flour.

Heat the oil with the butter in a large, heavy frying pan and sauté the slices quickly on both sides until tender and golden brown. Transfer them to a baking pan and season with salt and pepper.

Add the Marsala to the drippings remaining in the pan and cook for another minute or so, until mixture is slightly reduced, stirring the crusty bits from the bottom with a wooden spoon. Pour this mixture over the veal.

On each slice of veal place a slice of ham and a slice of cheese, or sprinkle the ham with Parmesan cheese.

Put into a 425° oven just long enough to melt the cheese.

Serves 6
Preparation Time:
 25 Minutes
Preheat oven to 425°

 2 lbs. veal fillets, cut into
   12 thin slices
   Flour for dredging
2½ Tbsps. olive oil
 3 Tbsps. butter
   Salt and pepper to
   taste
2½ Tbsps. Marsala wine
 12 slices ham
 12 slices mozzarella
   cheese or 5 Tbsps.
   grated Parmesan
   cheese

VINTAGE YEAR

Vintage Year
ECLECTIC CUISINE
405 Cloverdale Road
Montgomery, Alabama
(334) 264-8463
AVERAGE DINNER FOR TWO: $65

This trendy restaurant is located in a row of brick storefronts next to the historic Cloverdale residential area. The mix of condos, garage apartments and fine old homes make a perfect backdrop for Vintage Year's casual sophistication. The restaurant is a favorite spot for entertaining legislators, lobbyists and corporate guests.

Chef/owner Judy Martin's philosophy is to do "a few things very well" so diners are presented a menu that incorporates seasonal tastes and changes every two to three weeks. The menu can be influenced by Mexican, Italian and Pacific Rim cuisines. Known for well-prepared, fresh seafood, wonderful vegetarian dishes, superb sauces and innovative desserts, Chef Martin is an exciting member of Montgomery's culinary scene.

Menu teasers to try are the Chinese-Style Veal Dumplings in an Ancho Chile Sauce, Sautéed Shrimp with Scallions, Tomatoes, Garlic, Mushrooms, Feta Cheese and Pasta and the Grilled Tuna with a Mustard-Thyme Butter.

VINTAGE YEAR'S MENU FOR FOUR

Mesclun Salad with Orange Sage Vinaigrette

Roasted Double Lamb Chops with Fresh Herbs and Vegetables

Chocolate Bread Pudding

Mesclun Salad with Orange Sage Vinaigrette

Place sugar, sage, salt and pepper in a small bowl. Add vinegar and whisk until incorporated. Add orange juice concentrate and slowly add olive oil and mix well. Taste for seasoning and adjust.

Wash the mesclun greens gently. Drain and spin dry.

Place the greens in a salad bowl and toss with the vinaigrette. Garnish with orange zest.

Serves 4
Preparation Time:
  15 Minutes

  1 Tbsp. sugar
1½ tsps. fresh sage
  1 tsp. Kosher salt
  1 tsp. cracked pepper
  ¼ cup rice wine vinegar
  ¼ cup orange juice
    concentrate
  1 cup olive oil
  4 large handfuls
    mesclun,
    approximately ½ lb.
    Orange zest, garnish,
    optional

Roasted Double Lamb Chops with Fresh Herbs and Vegetables

Serves 4
Preparation Time:
  45 Minutes
(note marinating time)
Preheat oven to 350°

  2 Tbsps. fresh basil
  2 Tbsps. fresh rosemary, chopped
  2 Tbsps. fresh thyme, chopped
  ½ cup + 2 Tbsps. olive oil
  4 double lamb chops
  4 Tbsps. butter
  3 shallots, chopped
  6 Roma tomatoes, peeled, seeded, chopped
  2 cups veal stock
    Salt and pepper to taste
    Fresh herbs, such as thyme, basil, rosemary and flat leaf parsley
  5 shallots, chopped
  2 small carrots, sliced, parboiled
 12 pearl onions, parboiled
  8 small potatoes, roasted

Combine the basil, rosemary, thyme and ½ cup of olive oil and marinate lamb in mixture for about 2 hours.

Brown the lamb in the remaining 2 Tbsps. olive oil and 2 Tbsps. butter in a sauté pan. Transfer to a flat baking dish and roast in a 350° oven for about 12 minutes.

Pour the fat from the sauté pan and add the remaining 2 Tbsps. of butter and the shallots. Cook until translucent. Stir in the tomatoes and stock. Simmer for about 10 minutes. Add salt, pepper and fresh herbs. Add the vegetables. Heat until warm and serve over lamb.

Garnish with fresh basil and sprinkle with more herbs.

Chocolate Bread Pudding

Butter and line with buttered parchment paper 8 soufflé dishes, 6 oz. each. Set aside.

In a food processor, pulse together the chocolate, bread and 1 cup sugar until they are crumbs.

While the food processor is running, add 1½ cups hot cream, ½ cup butter, 1 tsp. vanilla and one egg at a time, until the mixture is smooth, for about 1 to 2 minutes.

Divide into the prepared soufflé dishes and bake in bain-marie or water-bath for 50 minutes in a 350° oven.

For the crème anglaise, beat together in a mixing bowl the egg yolks, remaining sugar, vanilla and salt until ribbons form.

Heat the remaining cream to scalding and slowly add to the egg mixture. Transfer the mixture to a heavy saucepan and cook over moderately low heat, stirring constantly with a wooden spoon until it begins to thicken.

Cool the sauce over an ice bath. Strain and refrigerate until ready to use.

For the chocolate sauce, melt the chocolate and cream together in a double boiler.

To serve, remove puddings from the soufflé dishes. Place on plates and top with crème anglaise and chocolate sauce.

Serves 4
Preparation Time:
1½ Hours
Preheat oven to 350°

½ cup (1 stick) unsalted butter + 1 Tbsp., cubed
1½ cups bittersweet chocolate, cut in small pieces
1 cup white bread, crusts removed
1⅔ cups sugar
4½ cups heavy cream, scalded
6 eggs
2 tsps. vanilla
9 egg yolks
Pinch of salt

Chocolate Sauce:
4 oz. bittersweet chocolate
¼ cup heavy cream

☆

VOYAGERS

Voyagers at the Perdido Beach Resort
GULF COAST CREOLE CUISINE
27200 Perdido Beach Boulevard
Orange Beach, Alabama
(205) 981-9811
Dinner Daily 5PM–10PM
AVERAGE DINNER FOR TWO: $55

ward-winning Chef Gerhard Wolfgang Brill creates an unparalleled experience at Voyagers at the Perdido Beach Resort. A favorite among locals and visitors alike, Voyagers greets diners with fine china and linen.

The menu is filled with fresh seafood and Chef Brill's unique and special creations. His creative interpretations of Creole specialties, using only the freshest ingredients, frequently vary from the conventional. Menu highlights include the famous Turtle Soup au Sherry, Filet of Red Snapper with Roasted Pecans in a Creole Meunière Sauce, Filet Mignon Stanley and Double French Amaretto Chocolate Slices served with Amaretto Cream.

VOYAGER'S MENU FOR FOUR

Turtle Soup au Sherry

Sautéed Shrimp en Pesto

Filet Mignon Stanley

Turtle Soup au Sherry

elt 1 cup butter in a heavy saucepan. Add the flour and cook, stirring frequently, over medium heat until the roux is a light brown. Set aside.

In a 5-qt. saucepan, melt the remaining butter and add the turtle meat. Cook over high heat until the meat is brown.

Add the celery, onions, garlic, seasoning and cook until vegetables are translucent.

Add the tomato purée, lower the heat and simmer for 10 minutes.

Add the stock and simmer 30 minutes.

Add the roux and cook over low heat, stirring until soup is smooth and thickened. Correct the seasoning to taste. Add the lemon, egg and spinach.

Remove from heat and serve. At the table, add 1 tsp. of sherry to each soup plate.

Cooking Secret: This soup is dark, thick and rich—a stew-type dish and filling enough to make a meal in itself.

Serves 4
Preparation Time:
  1 Hour

1½ cups butter, unsalted
  ¾ cup all-purpose flour
  3 lbs. turtle meat,
    ½-inch cubes
  1 cup celery, minced,
    about 4 stalks
1¼ cups onions, minced,
    about 2 medium-size
1½ tsps. garlic, minced
  3 bay leaves
  1 tsp. oregano
  ½ tsp. thyme
    Salt and black pepper
    to taste
  ⅛ tsp. cayenne pepper, or
    to taste
  ¼ tsp. salt, or to taste
1½ cups tomato purée
  1 qt. beef stock
  ½ lemon, seeds removed,
    finely chopped
  1 hard-cooked egg,
    finely chopped
  1 cup fresh spinach,
    minced
  4 tsps. dry sherry

★

Sautéed Shrimp en Pesto

Serves 4
Preparation Time:
30 Minutes

8 Tbsps. butter, unsalted
2 garlic cloves, minced
¼ Tbsp. basil
½ onion, diced
4 mushrooms, sliced
½ cup green onions,
   chopped
   Salt and black pepper
   to taste
⅛ tsp. cayenne pepper, or
   to taste
¼ cup shrimp stock
24 medium shrimp,
   peeled, deveined
½ cup dry white wine
½ oz. Romano cheese,
   grated

Melt 4 Tbsps. butter in a large saucepan and sauté the garlic, basil, onion, mushrooms, green onions, salt and peppers for 30 seconds, stirring gently. Add stock and simmer until onions are transparent. Add the shrimp and wine and simmer until liquid is almost evaporated.

Remove the pan from the heat and add the remaining butter and cheese, stirring gently until the butter is melted and the sauce is creamy.

Serve immediately.

☆

Filet Mignon

Bring the cream to a boil in a heavy saucepan over medium-high heat and boil rapidly until reduced to ⅓ its original quantity, or about ⅔ cup. Add a pinch of salt and pepper and stir in horseradish. Set aside and keep warm.

Sprinkle the filets with salt and peppers and sauté in 6 Tbsps. butter in a hot iron skillet for about 2 to 3 minutes on each side. While the filets are cooking, melt the remaining butter in a 9 × 12-inch baking pan.

Peel the bananas, cut lengthwise, and sauté them in the remaining butter with the curry powder until slightly soft.

To serve, place a heaping tablespoon of horseradish sauce on each plate, place a filet on top and garnish with 1 banana sliced in 4 pieces.

Serves 4
Preparation Time:
1 Hour

  2 cups heavy cream
    Salt to taste
    Freshly ground white
    pepper to taste
  3 Tbsps. fresh
    horseradish, shredded,
    not prepared
  4 filet mignon, 6 to 8 oz.
    each
    Salt and pepper to
    taste
  ¼ tsp. cayenne pepper, or
    to taste
 10 Tbsps. (1¼ sticks)
    butter
  4 bananas
  2 tsps. curry powder

MALAGA INN

Malaga Inn
359 Church Street
Mobile, Alabama 36602
(800) 235-1586
(334) 438-4701
ROOM RATES: $59–$135

T he Malaga Inn boasts a flair for Southern living at its best. Located in the historical district of downtown Mobile, the inn was originally two townhouses, built in 1862 by a couple of brothers-in-law "when the war was going well for the South."

The homes have been lovingly restored around a quiet patio and garden.

Guests may choose from among 40 rooms and suites, all decorated in Southern tradition and style with private baths and hardwood floors.

The garden landscape and gas-lit courtyard add to the romance and charm of this Southern destination.

Daikon with Caramelized Onions and Roasted Elephant Garlic

Cut the top off each garlic bulb and place them in a shallow roasting pan. Drizzle ¼ cup extra-virgin olive oil over the garlic bulbs and season with salt and pepper to taste. Roast in the oven at 350° for 20 minutes or until soft.

Sauté the onions in butter until caramelized. Remove from heat and allow to cool to room temperature.

Trim and peel the daikon radishes and cut into thirds. In a medium-sized sauce pot, braise the daikon in ¼ cup olive oil. Season with salt and pepper. When browned, deglaze with the white wine.

Add the caramelized onions, roasted garlic and vegetable stock. Reduce mixture by ¼ before serving.

Serves 4
Preparation Time:
  45 Minutes
Preheat oven to 350°

  4 **elephant garlic bulbs**
  ½ **cup extra-virgin olive oil**
     Salt and pepper to taste
  2 **onions, diced**
  2 **tsps. butter**
  4 **medium daikon radishes**
  1 **cup semi-sweet white wine**
  1 **cup vegetable stock**

☆

THE MENTONE INN

The Mentone Inn
6139 Highway 17
Mentone, Alabama 35984
(800) 455-7470
(205) 634-4836
ROOM RATES: $75–$125

Nestled atop Lookout Mountain, the Mentone Inn was built during the height of the roaring '20s. The beaded, hand-polished wood paneling and the gracious porch attest to its whimsical, adventuresome spirit, reflecting the bold era. This historic inn offers an outdoor hot tub surrounded by pristine forests and wildflowers as a relaxing retreat for its guests.

Mentone Inn is an easy drive from Atlanta, Birmingham, Hunstville or Chattanooga. Local attractions include Desoto State Park and Sequoyah Caverns, fishing and skiing. Miles of hiking trails are within minutes of the inn. Antiques and craft shops are a specialty of the Mentone area, along with a huge flea market.

Almond and Peach Macaroon Pie

I n a large bowl mix all ingredients together. Pour the mixture into a deep unbaked pie crust.

Bake at 250° or until the center is firm and the coconut is browned on top, approximately 1 to 1¼ hours.

Serves 6
Preparation Time:
  10 Minutes
Preheat oven to 250°

  1 cup milk
  4 eggs
1½ cups sugar
  1 cup white Karo
  1 stick butter, melted
  ¾ cup coconut
  ¾ cup almonds, sliced or
    1 tsp. almond extract
  3 packages (individual
    servings) peaches and
    cream instant oatmeal
  1 unbaked pie crust

TUTWILER HOTEL

Tutwiler Hotel
2021 Park Place North
Birmingham, Alabama 35203
(800) 845-1787
(205) 322-2100
ROOM RATES: $89–$172

An Alabama tradition since 1914, the award-winning Tutwiler Hotel offers luxury, history and Southern hospitality amid the glass and steel office towers and tourist attractions of Birmingham's vibrant downtown. History buffs and leisure travelers visit the eight-story red brick building to experience a bygone era when Warren G. Harding was President, Charles Lindbergh was an international hero and Will Rogers was a premier stage performer.

The Mobil Four-Star and AAA Four Diamond property features 147 guest rooms and suites, is furnished with original antiques, intricate masonry work, carved oak chandeliers and original marble tiles.

Christian's Restaurant, winner of Top 25 Restaurants In The Country by Best of the Best Dining Awards, features a menu combining the tastes of Europe, the Southeast and Alabama under the supervision of Executive Chef Bernard Axel. The restaurant is recognized for serving 30 different varieties of domestic and imported red and white wines by the glass each evening.

Poached Pears

Peel the pears, leaving them whole, with the stems intact.

In a large stock pot, bring the wine, water, sugar, cinnamon, cloves and ginger root to a boil, stirring until the sugar is dissolved. Add the pears and cook over low heat until tender.

Remove pears from the wine mixture. Refrigerate the pears, discarding the liquid. Serve pears chilled, either by themselves or on a bed of melted chocolate.

Serves 4
Preparation Time:
  15 Minutes
(note refrigeration time)

2 lbs. pears
2 cups red wine
1 cup water
2 cups sugar
2 cinnamon sticks
1 Tbsp. whole cloves
$\frac{1}{2}$ tsp. ginger or a few
  pieces of ginger root
1 lb. chocolate, melted,
  optional

GEORGIA:
Empire State
Of The South

The home of Uncle Remus and Scarlett O'Hara, Martin Luther King, Jr., and Pogo, Georgia is also the largest state east of the Mississippi River and the eleventh most populous in the United States. It encompasses the beginning of the Appalachian Trail and the Okefenokee Swamp, the Atlantic Seashore, the Blue Ridge Mountains and the Suwannee River, immortalized by Stephen Foster.

Early in Georgia's history, the Spanish and British clashed over the area. England prevailed, and in 1733, General James Oglethorpe was granted a charter to form a colony at Savannah. His plan, not entirely altruistic, was to transport imprisoned debtors to the new colony, where they could rehabilitate themselves through profitable labor—which, coincidentally, would financially benefit the proprietors of the colony. Alas, the plan failed, and twenty years later Oglethorpe and his trustees surrendered all power to the British government.

When white settlers headed West for Georgia's rich agricultural lands, Native Americans were dispossessed of their ancestral homelands. The Creeks and Cherokees were resettled beyond the Mississippi River in a forced relocation, which came to be known as the Trail of Tears. In 1828, gold was discovered near Dahlonega, sparking the nation's first gold rush.

In January 1861, Georgia, the fourth of the original 13 states, seceded. The Civil War in Georgia began and ended in Savannah. A rich, confident state at the beginning of the war, by the time General William Tecumseh Sherman smashed through the state on his devastating march to the sea, 80 percent of Georgia's wealth and a majority of its young men had disappeared. Georgia was readmitted to the Union in 1870.

A view of Savannah, 1855

Photo from the Hargrett Rare Book and Manuscript Library, University of Georgia Libraries

Today, Georgia is first in the nation in pulpwood production, turpentine, resin, peanuts and pecans; and second in broiling chickens and eggs. Four hundred of the Fortune 500 companies have offices in Atlanta, and Coca Cola, CNN, UPS and the American Cancer Society are headquartered in this most forward-looking of Southern cities. The National Center for Disease Control is also situated in Atlanta.

Georgia's recreational facilities include the luxurious resorts on the Golden Isles—Sea Island, Jekyll and St. Simons—quiet backwood trails, mountaineering and river rafting. And, of course, it was "Georgia On My Mind" (incidentally, the state song) for hundreds of millions of people around the world as they caught the fever of the 1996 Summer Olympic Games in Atlanta.

James Bowie, James Brown, Erskine Caldwell, Jimmy Carter, Ray Charles, Ty Cobb, John C. Fremont, Joel Chandler Harris, Martin Luther King, Jr., Gladys Knight, Margaret Mitchell, Flannery O'Connor, Otis Redding, Jackie Robinson and Alice Walker have called Georgia their home.

Here are some of the highlights of a trip to Georgia.

ANDERSONVILLE NATIONAL HISTORIC SITE was the most infamous prison of the Civil War. Built to accommodate 10,000 prisoners, it eventually confined more than three times that number. The poverty-stricken Confederate government was unable even to feed the prisoners, and the mortality rate was unbelievable. At the end of the war, the prison commandant was convicted by a military tribunal and hanged.

ATLANTA is the diadem in the crown of Georgia. Yet despite its soaring skyscrapers, it has never lost its distinctive Southern charm. The CNN STUDIO TOUR takes you inside the nerve center of the world, while THE WORLD OF COCA COLA lets you listen to radio jingles and view history at an old-time soda fountain. The MARTIN LUTHER KING, JR., NATIONAL HISTORIC SITE commemorates the life and deeds of the fallen civil rights leader and the ATLANTA HISTORY CENTER not only allows you to re-enter the pre-Civil War life of the South, but gives you "time out" with 32 acres of gardens and woodland trails so you might relax, away from the roar of the big city.

STONE MOUNTAIN, just outside of Atlanta, is a magnificent destination that will keep you entertained for an

Benning Gold Mine on the Yahoola River in northeastern Georgia

Photo from the Hargrett Rare Book and Manuscript Library, University of Georgia Libraries.

entire day. There's the ANTEBELLUM PLANTATION, the ANTIQUE CAR AND TREASURE MUSEUM, a riverboat cruise on the Scarlett O'Hara, a scenic old-time railroad and a CABLE CAR RIDE to the summit of Stone Mountain, a 300-million-year-old massive granite dome rising 825 above the floor of the valley. Finally, for kids of all ages, there's the WILDLIFE PRESERVE AND PETTING FARM.

For Civil War buffs, there's **CHICKAMAUGA AND CHATTANOOGA NATIONAL MILITARY PARK,** whose 8,100 acres straddle both Georgia and Tennessee. Several areas within the park commemorate Civil War battles—there are more than 1,500 tablets, monuments and cannons showing the battle lines.

Although **DAHLONEGA** today is a sleepy town of 3,100 people, it was the first boom town in America when, in 1828, gold fever swept a wave of fortune hunters to the area. You can pan for the precious metal at Blackburn Park, Old Dahlonega and Crisson Mines. Good luck!

The subtropical **GOLDEN ISLES** include the CUMBERLAND ISLAND NATIONAL SEASHORE, FORT FREDERICA NATIONAL MONUMENT and the romantic, upscale haunts of

The Jekyll Island Club

old-time millionaires at JEKYLL ISLAND, ST. SIMONS ISLAND, SAPELO ISLAND and SEA ISLAND.

If you *really* want to go back in history, you can't beat **OCMULGEE NATIONAL MONUMENT,** 700 acres of the most impressive American-Indian mounds in the Southeast,

Photo from the Hargrett Rare Book and Manuscript Library, University of Georgia Libraries

encompassing the period from 10,000 B.C. through the early 19th century.

SAVANNAH, with a population of just over 140,000, was Georgia's first city, and its most historically significant. A lost fight to save the old vegetable and fish market in the early 1950s served as a "wake-up call" to preserve this charming old bastion of Southern hospitality. Today, 22 of General Oglethorpe's original 24 town squares survive. River Street's Waving Girl statue commemorates a young girl who promised her sailor sweetheart to wave to every ship coming into port until he returned to her. Don't miss the SAVANNAH TOUR OF HOMES AND GARDENS: one of the homes you'll visit is the birthplace of Juliette Gordon Low, founder of the Girl Scouts. In the SAVANNAH HISTORY MUSEUM, located on the site of a Revolutionary War battle, you'll see a model of the S.S. *Savannah,* the first steamship to cross the Atlantic (1809), an 1890 Baldwin locomotive, a cotton gin and one of the Oscars awarded to songwriter Johnny Mercer, a Savannah native. While you're here, don't forget to take a Savannah Riverboat cruise.

The **GEORGIA AGRIRAMA** at Tifton is a 95-acre living history museum. You enter the life of an 1890s town, complete with farmsteading communities and costumed interpreters, who make this a most special place.

Franklin Delano Roosevelt, our nation's only four-term president, spent what leisure time he had in Warm Springs, known for centuries for its curative powers. He spent his last days here and died in the **LITTLE WHITE HOUSE STATE HISTORIC SITE**—today, a memorial shrine. Walk along a path lined with stones and flags from all 50 states and you'll come to a museum chronicling Roosevelt's life and his place in history.

The **WARNER ROBBINS MUSEUM OF AVIATION** contains more than 85 historical aircraft, housed in four buildings and a hangar. There's a MIG-17 here, a cutaway replica of a B-17 and numerous World War II aircraft. Enter the flight simulator to experience a highly realistic fighting mission.

The **OKEFENOKEE SWAMP** is more than just Pogo's home. It's a 1,600-acre wildlife sanctuary highlighted by flower gardens, wilderness trails, observation towers and a 1½-mile boat tour of Native American waterways.

BACCHANALIA

Bacchanalia
NEW AMERICAN CUISINE
3125 Piedmont Road
Atlanta, Georgia
(404) 365-0410
Dinner Tuesday–Saturday 6PM–11PM
AVERAGE DINNER FOR TWO: $80

A twisted path led Bacchanalia chef-owners Anne Quatrano from Connecticut and Cliff Harrison from Hawaii to the rolling hills of North Georgia, where they grow the produce served in their popular Atlanta restaurant.

Together they transformed a local antique shop, on busy Piedmont Road in Atlanta, into a beguiling cottage serving prix-fixe dinners with such culinary winners as Maine Lobster and Yukon Gold Potato Ravioli, Organic Squash Soup with Roasted Pumpkin Seed Oil, Pepper- and Thyme-Cured Beef Tenderloin with Caramelized Sweet Onions and Maple Pecan Tart. Their philosophy is simple. They like to build on good strong flavors, but still try to keep it light.

Using family heirlooms such as silver, candles and gauzy drapes hanging from golden rods, the restaurant atmosphere is comfortable and casual. Consistently voted one of Atlanta's best dining spots, Bacchanalia's menu is influenced by the couples' love for California, using the freshest ingredients and a wine list to satisfy even the most serious connoisseur.

BACCHANALIA'S MENU FOR FOUR

Butternut Squash Soup with Roasted Pumpkin Seed Oil

Grilled Quail with Spicy Creamed Collard Greens

Roast Beets with Fresh Goat Cheese

Maple Pecan Tart with Chocolate Sorbet

Butternut Squash Soup with Roasted Pumpkin Seed Oil

Pour the chicken stock into a large pot and add the cubed squash. Bring to a boil and cook until tender. Do not overcook. Purée and strain. Season with salt and pepper and reheat slowly in a large pot. Add the cream.

Before serving, swirl in the butter. Do not bring the soup to a boil during the second reheating. If you wish the soup to be thicker, add cornstarch mixed with cold water during the reheating process.

Drizzle with a few drops of the roasted pumpkin seed oil before serving.

Serves 4
Preparation Time:
45 Minutes

6 cups chicken stock
2 large butternut squash, peeled, cubed
Salt and pepper to taste
$\frac{1}{4}$ cup heavy cream
1 Tbsp. butter
3 Tbsps. cornstarch, optional
Austrian roasted pumpkin seed oil (available at international markets)

☆

Grilled Quail with Spicy Creamed Collard Greens

Serves 4
Preparation Time:
  45 Minutes

- 1 smoked ham hock or ½ tsp. liquid smoke
- 2 tsps. + 1 dash green Tabasco
- ½ cup white vinegar
- ¼ cup + 1 Tbsp. maple syrup
  Salt and ground pepper to taste
- 2 lbs. fresh baby collard greens, stemmed
- ½ cup chicken stock or broth
- ¼ cup heavy cream
- 1 dash hot pepper vinegar
- 1 Tbsp. roast garlic purée
- 1 Tbsp. Wondra (finely milled flour)
- 4 semi-boneless quail
- 1 Tbsp. olive oil
  Smoked bacon, cooked, finely diced for garnish

In a hot, large pot, sear the ham hock. Then add 1 gallon water and add 2 tsps. Tabasco, liquid smoke (if not using the ham hock), vinegar, ¼ cup maple syrup and salt. Bring to a boil. Adjust the seasonings.

Blanch the collard greens in this mixture for about 2 minutes until soft and tender in texture but still green. Remove from water and let cool. Slice into ½-inch strips.

To serve, heat ½ cup chicken stock, heavy cream, a dash of hot pepper vinegar, 1 dash green Tabasco, 1 Tbsp. maple syrup, 1 Tbsp. roast garlic purée and salt and pepper to taste. Heat to a boil and sprinkle with Wondra. Cook until slightly thick. Add the cooked collard greens. Keep warm.

Brush the quail with a small amount of olive oil, salt and pepper. Grill on a hot grill for about 6 minutes on each side. Do not overcook.

Serve the collard greens in a large bowl with the grilled quail on top. Garnish with diced bacon.

Roast Beets with Fresh Goat Cheese

I n a bowl, whisk together the shallots, ¼ cup raspberry vinegar and most of the honey. Drizzle in the oil slowly and season with salt and pepper to taste. Do not be shy with the salt and pepper. Set aside.

Trim the ends of the beets and place in a deep baking dish. Fill with water to halfway cover the beets. Add a small drizzle of honey, ¼ cup raspberry vinegar, butter, salt and pepper. Cover with aluminum foil and bake in a 350° oven for approximately 45 minutes.

To serve, sandwich the goat cheese between the beets and drizzle with the vinaigrette. We serve this as a salad or cheese course after the main meal.

Cooking Secret: The cooking time varies greatly depending on the type, age and freshness of the beets. To check for doneness, rub the skin of the beet. If it freely falls off the beet, they are done. We like our beets to remain slightly firm, yet cooked. Peel while hot and slice into the vinaigrette. Let cool.

Serves 4
Preparation Time:
  1 Hour
Preheat oven to 350°

  1 **medium shallot, finely**
     diced
 ½ **cup raspberry vinegar**
 ¼ **cup honey**
 ¼ **cup grapeseed oil**
     Salt and cracked black
     pepper to taste
  4 **small beets, about**
     2 inches in diameter
     Water
  1 **Tbsp. butter**
  4 **oz. fresh goat cheese**

☆

Maple Pecan Tart

Yield:
  4 individual tarts
Preparation Time:
  45 Minutes
(note refrigeration time)
Preheat oven to 325°

9½ Tbsps. butter, cold
3 Tbsps. powdered sugar
1 egg yolk
¾ cup flour
1½ tsps. heavy cream
  Pinch of salt
2 eggs
⅓ cup sugar
¼ cup maple syrup
¼ cup Karo syrup
  Pinch of salt
2 cups pecans, toasted, roughly chopped

For the tart crust, cream 6½ Tbsps. butter and the powdered sugar together in a large mixing bowl. Add the egg yolk. Add half the flour. Then add the heavy cream, remaining flour and salt. Mix until the dough just comes together. Form a ball and refrigerate for at least 1 hour. Roll dough to ¼-inch thickness and fill the tart shells. Freeze for 30 minutes and bake at 325° for 13 minutes.

Combine the eggs, sugar, maple syrup, Karo syrup and salt in a mixing bowl. Add 3 Tbsps. melted butter. Fill each cooked tart shell with pecans. Cover with the egg mixture and bake in a 325° oven until set, about 20 minutes. Serve the tarts warm with a scoop of chocolate sorbet (recipe follows).

Chocolate Sorbet

Bring the water, orange juice, sugar, corn syrup and cocoa powder to a boil in a large pot. Simmer for 3 minutes.

Add the chocolate and stir until dissolved.

Strain and chill. Freeze following instructions in your ice cream freezer manual.

Serves 4
Preparation Time:
  10 Minutes
(note refrigeration time)

  5 cups water
    Juice from 2 oranges
2½ cups sugar
  ½ cup corn syrup
  ½ cup cocoa powder
  6 oz. bittersweet
    chocolate

☆

BONE'S

Bone's
AMERICAN CUISINE
3130 Piedmont Road N.E.
Atlanta, Georgia
(404) 237-2663
Lunch Monday–Friday 11:30AM–2:30PM
Dinner Daily 6PM–11PM
AVERAGE DINNER FOR TWO: $90

Bone's, voted "Best Steak House in Atlanta" for most of its 19 years, has retained most of its traditions while growing in new directions by offering more seafood, new Southern dishes, spa options and a new wine gallery.

The steaks are opulent here, with a concentrated flavor of tender, corn-fed, aged beef. The ultimate encounter comes in the form of a T-bone. You can expect all the classic cuts, grilled to order, served without flourish. Bone's has always been famous for its huge lobsters. The range of seafood has expanded to include, among other items, Hickory Grilled Swordfish with a Tomato and Roasted Red Pepper Compote and Seared Salmon with Scallion Chutney and Citrus-Balsamic Vinaigrette. Vegetarians need not feel out of place at Bone's, for they will find enough deliciously prepared vegetables to feast upon. There are some good desserts on the menu such as Pecan Pie, Chiffon Cheesecake and Mile-High Ice Cream Pie with a Sweet Brownie Crust.

BONE'S MENU FOR SIX

Bone's Salad

Seared Salmon with Garlic Vinaigrette and Radish Slaw

Grit Fritters in Horseradish and Country Ham Beurre Blanc

Bone's Salad

Prepare the vinaigrette in a medium-sized mixing bowl. Combine the egg yolk, mustard, salt, pepper, sugar, oregano, basil and vinegar. Slowly whisk in the vegetable oil. Set aside.

Core the apples, slicing each into 8 pieces. Sprinkle with cinnamon and set aside.

In a large bowl, put the lettuce and pistachios and toss with raspberry vinaigrette. Divide onto 6 chilled plates.

Place four apple slices around each salad. Sprinkle with grated Stilton and serve chilled.

Cooking Secret: The vinaigrette can be made ahead.

Serves 6
Preparation Time:
  20 Minutes

  1 egg yolk
  1 Tbsp. Dijon mustard
  ½ tsp. salt
  ¼ tsp. white pepper
  3 tsps. sugar
  ½ tsp. oregano
  ½ tsp. basil
  ¼ cup raspberry vinegar
  ¾ cup vegetable oil
  3 Granny Smith apples
  1 tsp. cinnamon
  5 heads Bibb lettuce,
      washed, dried
  ¾ cup pistachio pieces,
      toasted
  ½ cup Stilton cheese,
      grated

Seared Salmon with Garlic Vinaigrette and Radish Slaw

Serves 6
Preparation Time:
  45 Minutes
(note refrigeration time)

  2 Tbsps. garlic purée
  2 Tbsps. Dijon mustard
  ¼ cup white Balsamic
    vinegar
  ¾ cup olive oil
  ½ cup salad oil
  ¼ tsp. black pepper
  1 tsp. salt
  2 Tbsps. parsley,
    chopped
  1 cup radishes, julienned
  2 Tbsps. olive oil
  1 Tbsp. champagne
    vinegar
  ½ tsp. sugar
    Salt and cayenne
    pepper to taste
  6 salmon filets, 4 oz.
    each

I n a medium-sized mixing bowl, combine the garlic, mustard and vinegar, mixing well. Slowly add in ½ cup olive oil and salad oil. Blend well. Season with the pepper, salt and parsley. Chill over night.

For the slaw, combine the radishes, 2 Tbsps. olive oil, champagne vinegar and sugar together in a mixing bowl. Season to taste with salt and pepper and chill for 1 hour.

Heat a medium sauté pan. Brush the salmon filets with ¼ cup olive oil, sprinkle with salt and pepper and sear face-side down until golden brown. Turn over and brown the other side, about 5 minutes.

Serve the salmon drizzled with the garlic vinaigrette and the radish slaw.

Grit Fritters in Horseradish and Country Ham Beurre Blanc

In a medium-sized saucepan, bring the water to a boil. Slowly add the grits and simmer until all the water is absorbed, about 15 minutes over a very low heat, stirring occasionally. Cool slightly. Stir in the cheese, salt and white pepper. Remove the pan from the heat and allow to cool for 30 minutes or until grits are firm. Stir in the chives. While grits are cooling, prepare the beurre blanc.

In a small saucepan, reduce the white wine and shallots to 1 Tbsp. Stir in the cream and reduce by half. In a small cup, mix the cornstarch with ½ Tbsp. water and stir into the cream mixture. On high heat, whisking constantly, add the butter, a few cubes at a time, until all the butter has been incorporated and the sauce is thick. Strain into a container. Stir in the country ham, red pepper and horseradish. Set aside and keep warm.

Use a tablespoon to form fritter mixture into oval balls. Dredge lightly in flour. Heat oil in a deep-fat fryer or skillet to 350°. Fry the fritters until golden brown on all sides.

Place the beurre blanc on serving plates and top with fritters. Garnish with chopped parsley and serve.

Serves 6
Preparation Time:
45 Minutes

- 1 qt. water
- 1 cup quick-cooking grits
- 11 oz. Boursin cheese
- ½ tsp. salt
- ⅛ tsp. white pepper
- ⅓ cup chives, chopped
- 1 cup white wine
- 1½ Tbsps. shallots, minced
- ½ cup heavy cream
- ½ tsp. cornstarch
- ½ lb. unsalted butter, cubed into 1-inch cubes, softened
- 1½ Tbsps. country ham, cooked, thinly diced
- 1½ Tbsps. red pepper, roasted, thinly diced
- 2½ tsps. horseradish
  Flour for dredging
  Oil for deep frying
  Parsley, chopped, for garnish

★

BUCKHEAD DINER

Buckhead Diner
AMERICAN CUISINE
3073 Piedmont Road
Atlanta, Georgia
(404) 262-3336
Lunch and Dinner Monday–Saturday 11AM–Midnight
Lunch and Dinner Sunday 11AM–10PM
AVERAGE DINNER FOR TWO: $45

Seldom has a restaurant instigated such enthusiasm as this gourmet eatery—Atlanta embraced the concept immediately and has yet to lower its excitement. The modern American cuisine highlights original snacks, novelty signature sandwiches, grilled specials, fresh seafood, fun desserts, plus creative yet identifiable diner foods. A few of the popular menu items include Crispy Salt and Pepper Calamari, Veal Meatloaf with Wild Mushrooms and Celery-Mashed Potatoes and White Chocolate Banana Cream Pie.

A custom creation from the renowned design firm of Kuleto Consulting and Design (based in Sausalito, California), the Buckhead Diner is reminiscent of a great Orient Express rail car. It has an exterior sheathed in a skin of radiantly polished stainless steel; a checkered board of black, white and cobalt blue porcelain enamel; and a fiery glow of multi-colored neon lighting. The floors sport an optic design fashioned in three tones of imported Italian marble. The kitchen has an open-style layout. The bar area is an important element of the restaurant, and its granite counter tops are polished to a high luster, which is accentuated by special lighting. Custom booths are detailed with rich fabrics and delicate hand-laid marquetry made from exotic hardwoods.

BUCKHEAD DINER'S MENU FOR SIX

Veal Meatloaf with Wild Mushrooms

Peach Bread Pudding

White Chocolate Banana Cream Pie

Veal Meatloaf with Wild Mushrooms

C lean the mushrooms. Cut white mushrooms and shiitakes into quarters. Cut the oyster mushrooms into thirds.

Sauté the garlic and shallots in butter until clear. Add the mushrooms and cook until tender. Allow to cool

In a bowl, mix the bread crumbs with the cream, herbs, mustard and eggs. Add mixture to ground veal. Mix well and season with salt, pepper and Worcestershire.

Form into a loaf on a baking sheet. Bake at 350° for 45 minutes or until juices run clear.

Serves 6
Preparation Time:
 1 Hour
Preheat oven to 350°

- ¼ lb. white mushrooms
- ¼ lb. shiitake mushrooms
- ¼ lb. oyster mushrooms
- 1 tsp. garlic, chopped
- ½ Tbsp. shallots
- 1 Tbsp. butter
- ¾ cup white bread crumbs
- ⅓ cup heavy cream
- ¼ bunch parsley, minced
- ¼ bunch thyme, leaves only
- ¼ bunch chives, minced
- 4 Tbsps. Dijon mustard
- 3 eggs
- 2½ lbs. ground veal
  Salt and fresh ground pepper to taste
- 1 Tbsp. Worcestershire sauce

Peach Bread Pudding

Serves 6
Preparation Time:
 40 Minutes
Preheat oven to 350°

   1 loaf egg bread
   2 Tbsps. butter, melted
   2 cups cinnamon sugar
   5 eggs
   1 cup sugar
 $\frac{1}{2}$ tsp. cinnamon
 $1\frac{1}{2}$ cups half and half
 $1\frac{1}{2}$ cups heavy or
      whipping cream
   2 16 oz. cans peaches in
      juice
   2 fluid oz. peach brandy
      Whipped cream for
      garnish

Cut egg bread into 1-inch cubes and toss them with the butter and cinnamon sugar. Place in the oven for 4 to 6 minutes or until golden brown.

Whisk eggs, sugar and cinnamon in bowl until pale.

Bring half and half cream to a boil and add to the egg mixture. Strain into $1\frac{1}{2}$ cups of heavy cream. Set aside.

Strain peaches from juice. Purée $\frac{1}{3}$ of the peaches and cut the remaining $\frac{2}{3}$ of the peaches into large pieces.

Add the peach purée and pieces to the egg mixture.

Put the toasted bread cubes in a large bowl and mix with peach-egg mixture and add the peach brandy.

Use six 12 oz. soufflé cups or a large gratin bowl. Butter the cups and coat with cinnamon sugar. Fill them generously with the bread pudding mixture.

Bake for 25 to 30 minutes in 350° oven.

Serve warm topped with whipped cream.

White Chocolate Banana Cream Pie

Whisk together the egg, sugar and cornstarch. Bring the half and half to a boil. Slowly add the egg mixture while whisking constantly. Return to low heat and whisk constantly, returning to a boil and thickening mixture. Remove from heat and whisk in the white chocolate. Pour the mixture into a bowl and sprinkle with powdered sugar. Set aside to cool.

Set aside the pre-baked 10-inch pie crust.

Whip the cream with the sugar until soft peaks form. Fold in the pastry cream lightly and add the banana pieces. Add the liqueur, being careful not to over-blend the ingredients. Fill the pie crust with the mixture. Cover with the white chocolate shavings and sprinkle with cocoa powder.

Yield:
  One 10-inch pie
Preparation Time:
  45 Minutes

  1 egg
2½ Tbsps. sugar
  1 Tbsp. cornstarch
  ¾ cup half and half
  2 oz. white chocolate
     Powdered sugar for
     dusting
     Pre-baked 10-inch pie
     crust
  2 cups heavy cream
  ½ cup sugar
1½ cups pastry cream
  1 ripe banana, cut in
     6 pieces
  1 Tbsp. banana liqueur
  1 Tbsp. white chocolate,
     shaved
  1 Tbsp. cocoa powder

☆

CITY GRILL

City Grill
CONTEMPORARY AMERICAN CUISINE
50 Hurt Plaza, Suite 200
Atlanta, Georgia
(404) 524-2489
Lunch Monday–Friday 11:30AM–2:30PM
Dinner Monday–Saturday 5:30PM–10PM
AVERAGE DINNER FOR TWO: $70

T o keep up with changing times and tastes, the City Grill lowered its prices and updated its look without giving up the luxurious starched linens, real silver, fantasy-landscape murals and superior selection of big red wines that were part of its original appeal. Whether it is a power lunch or a romantic dinner, this restaurant delivers, with its opulent decor of gold curtains, marble pillars and a grand staircase. It feels like a cross between the first-class lounge of the Queen Mary and a Philadelphia men's club.

Chef Roger Kaplan creates original Southwestern and Southern dishes that are tasty and healthy. Fitness Magazine named him one of America's Healthiest Chefs. Cooking is very seasonal and menus change often, but regulars keep coming back to try whatever's new. Diners are delighted by the Wood Grilled Alaskan BBQ Salmon, Wild Mushroom Ravioli and Hickory Fired Swordfish. With choices such as Coca-Cola Cake, Raspberry Bavarian Cake and Peach and Blackberry Crackle, diners are tempted to go directly to the desserts.

CITY GRILL'S MENU FOR FOUR

Pan-Fried Soft-Shell Crab with Lobster Slaw and Yellow Tomato Vinaigrette

Roasted Vidalia Onion Salad with Baby Lettuces and Orange Bacon Vinaigrette

Pan Seared Salmon on Vidalia Onion Potato Cake with Caviar Sauce

Warm Chocolate Pecan Soufflé Cake with Chocolate Sauce

Pan-Fried Soft-Shell Crab with Lobster Slaw and Yellow Tomato Vinaigrette

F or the lobster slaw, combine the lobster meat, cabbage, spinach, carrots, tomatoes, onions, lime and lemon juice, zest, oil, salt and pepper in a large mixing bowl. Toss together well. Set aside.

Clean the crabs by removing the gills, tails and intestines. Cut crabs in half.

Combine flour, salt and black pepper. Dredge the crab in the seasoned flour, then coat shells in buttermilk and dredge them back into the flour. Coat well.

Heat oil in pan to moderate heat. Add crabs and cook until golden brown on both sides. Remove from heat to absorbent paper.

To serve, place about 4 Tbsps. of the yellow tomato vinaigrette on each of 4 serving plates. Place the whole soft-shell crabs, belly side up, on the center of the plate. Stand up the half soft-shell crabs, two per plate, with the legs standing up in the air.

Divide the lobster slaw evenly among the 4 plates, placing it between the soft-shell halves and piling it high. Garnish each plate with 2 chive sticks.

Serves 4
Preparation Time:
  45 Minutes

½ cup cooked lobster
  meat, ¼-inch dice
5 cups cabbage, finely
  shredded
1 cup spinach, finely
  shredded
¼ cup carrots, julienned
  fine
¼ cup red tomatoes,
  julienned
¼ cup red onions,
  julienned
  Juice from ½ lime
  Juice and zest from
  1 lemon
2 Tbsps. canola oil
  Salt and black pepper
  to taste
8 soft-shell crabs
4 cups flour
3 cups buttermilk
  Canola oil for pan-
  frying
  Yellow Tomato
  Vinaigrette (recipe
  follows)
8 chive sticks, garnish

★

Yellow Tomato Vinaigrette

**Preparation Time:
45 Minutes**

1 Tbsp. garlic, minced
1 onion, roughly
  chopped
2 Tbsps. celery, roughly
  chopped
1 shallot, sliced
1 Tbsp. canola oil
½ cup white wine
4 yellow tomatoes,
  roughly chopped
½ cup water
1 tsp. thyme
1 Tbsp. basil
  Salt and black pepper
  to taste
1 tsp. champagne
  vinegar
½ cup canola oil

Sauté the garlic, onions, celery and shallots in canola oil until tender. Deglaze, using white wine. Reduce until liquid is almost gone.

Add the tomatoes and water. Simmer until tomatoes are soft and cooked, approximately 25 minutes.

Add thyme, basil, salt, black pepper and champagne vinegar.

Place in a blender. Blend until smooth and add the canola oil slowly until it is emulsified.

Chill.

Cooking Secret: The yellow tomato vinaigrette can be made up to 2 days ahead and kept in the refrigerator.

★

Roasted Vidalia Onion Salad with Baby Lettuces and Orange Bacon Vinaigrette

Peel and cut out ⅔ of the root of the onion while leaving the onion intact. Too much cut out will result in the onions breaking apart.

Coat onions and season with salt and pepper.

Roast in 300° oven until tender but not soft, approximately 2 hours. Let cool.

Peel off outer layer of onion and cut out core leaving a ½-inch diameter hole.

Using the next 2 layers, cut 6 petals from each, alternating petals like a flower. Place lettuce bundle in center of the onion. Serve on a bed of lettuce, garnished with arugula and vinaigrette.

Serves 4
Preparation Time:
  2½ Hours
Preheat oven to 300°

  4 **medium Vidalia**
    onions
    Salt and pepper to
    taste
  ¼ **cup extra virgin olive**
    oil
  3 **lbs. mixed lettuce**
    (red oak, red or green
    romaine, etc.)
  ¼ **lb. arugula**
    Orange bacon
    vinaigrette (recipe
    follows)

☆

Orange Bacon Vinaigrette

Preparation Time:
  15 Minutes
(note refrigeration time)

  2 **oranges, skinned,**
     sliced
     Zest from 2 oranges
1½ **cups rice wine vinegar**
  2 **Tbsps. apple-smoked**
     bacon, diced
     Juice from 1 orange
 ¾ **cup canola oil**
  1 **shallot, minced**
     Salt and pepper to
     taste

Place the oranges, zest and rice wine vinegar in a saucepan. Bring to a slow boil for 5 minutes. Remove from the heat but allow to stay warm for 2 hours. Then chill.

Discard the orange pulp and zest from the vinegar. Set aside the orange-vinegar.

Cut bacon into small dice and cook out fat over medium heat. Bacon should be crisp. Remove and place on paper towels to remove excess fat. Discard the fat.

Mix all orange-vinegar mixture and bacon with remaining ingredients.

Pan-Seared Salmon on Vidalia Onion Potato Cake with Caviar Sauce

I n a saucepan with oil, brown the shrimp shells for 3 to 4 minutes. Do not burn. Reduce the heat and add the onions, celery and leeks. Sweat until clear. Add half of each herb and the white wine and reduce until mixture is dry. Add the stock and simmer for 15 to 20 minutes.

Mix together the cornstarch and the water and add to sauce to thicken. Let sauce cook for 10 minutes more. Strain and press thorough a fine sieve. Season with salt and pepper to taste.

Add caviars, lemon zest and chives right before serving. Garnish with remaining herbs.

Serves 4
Preparation Time:
  45 Minutes
Yield:
  1½ qts.

Caviar Sauce:
  1 Tbsp. canola oil
  ¼ cup shrimp shells, raw
  1 onion, medium
    chopped
  1 celery stalk, medium
    chopped
  1 leek, medium chopped
  2 sprigs basil
  2 sprigs thyme
  2 sprigs Italian parsley
  ¼ cup white wine
  1½ cups chicken stock
    Cornstarch to thicken,
    as needed
    Water, as needed
    Salt and pepper to
    taste
  ½ oz. salmon roe
  ½ oz. trout roe
  ½ oz. whitefish roe
  ½ oz. orange tobiko
  ½ oz. black tobiko
  1 Tbsp. lemon zest
  1 Tbsp. chives, minced
    Potato cake (recipe
    follows)

Potato Cake

Preparation Time:
45 Minutes

- **4 potatoes, peeled,
  shredded, rinsed to
  remove excess starch
  Salt and pepper to
  taste**
- **4 oz. cream cheese**
- **2 Tbsps. shiitake
  mushrooms, julienned**
- **4 Tbsps. Vidalia onions,
  julienned**
- **2 Tbsps. clarified butter**
- **4 salmon filets, 6 oz.
  each**
- **1 cup spinach, minced,
  sautéed**

I n a sauté pan on low to medium heat, place rings or molds. Add half of the shredded potatoes in the rings and season with salt and pepper.

Mix cream cheese, mushrooms and onions. Add the mixture to each ring on top of the potatoes.

Ladle a small amount of butter over potatoes. Fill rings with remaining potatoes and flip over, adding more butter.

When potatoes are golden in color and have a good crust, transfer to sheet pan and remove rings, trimming off excess potato.

Sear salmon on both sides, being sure it has good coloring on top side.

On a large oval platter, place a potato cake in the center with sautéed spinach on top. Place salmon on top of spinach. Pour the caviar sauce around potato cake.

☆

Warm Chocolate Pecan Soufflé Cake with Chocolate Sauce

Melt 4 Tbsps. butter and paint four soufflé cups with butter. Coat the inside of each cup with 2 Tbsps. of chopped pecans.

Melt the chocolate and 10 Tbsps. butter together. Set aside.

Whip the egg yolks, 4 Tbsps. sugar and the brown sugar together in a large mixing bowl until mixture is well blended. Fold the egg mixture into the chocolate mixture. Fold the almond flour and the all-purpose flour into the chocolate mixture.

Whip the egg whites and the remaining sugar until soft peaks form. Fold the whipped egg whites into the chocolate mixture. Fill each of the 4 cups with 1 cup of the batter.

Bake at 325° for 45 minutes. Unmold when cool. Leave out at room temperature if you are serving them that day. If you are baking a day ahead, wrap and store in refrigerator.

Serve the soufflé warm with the chocolate sauce.

For the sauce, chop the chocolate into 1-inch sized chunks.

Bring the cream to a boil. Once boiled, remove from heat. Pour cream over chocolate chunks and whisk until smooth. Hold warm or refrigerate until ready to use. Reheat slowly.

Serves 4
Preparation Time:
 1½ Hours
Preheat oven to 325°

Soufflé:
 14 **Tbsps. butter**
 ¼ **lb. pecans, chopped**
 7 **oz. chocolate**
 10 **egg yolks**
 ½ **cup sugar**
 4 **Tbsps. brown sugar**
 2 **Tbsps. almond flour**
 2 **Tbsps. all-purpose**
   flour
 10 **egg whites**

Chocolate Sauce:
 10 **oz. chocolate**
 ¾ **cup heavy cream**

☆

ELIZABETH ON 37TH

Elizabeth on 37th
NEW SOUTHERN CUISINE
105 East 37th Street
Savannah, Georgia
(912) 236-5547
Dinner Monday–Saturday 6PM–10:30PM
AVERAGE DINNER FOR TWO: $90

Elizabeth on 37th, the creation of Chef Elizabeth Terry and her husband, wine steward Michael, weaves a romantic web around many diners. The simple elegance of their turn-of-the-century Southern mansion sets the perfect tone for her subtle and stunning new regional cooking based on wonderful old Southern recipes. Her secret is serving simply prepared, perfectly fresh, innovative dishes in the Southern tradition. Working with local farmers, Chef Terry encourages them to grow a variety of vegetables, including purple okra and green okra, so that she can create different dishes.

Menu highlights include a Tart brimming with Blue Crab, Mushroom, Tomato and Cheese, a Spicy Savannah Red Rice with Georgia Shrimp, Broiled Mustard-Garlic Glazed Salmon with a Grilled Curry Eggplant with Turnip and Pepper and a Pecan and Almond Tart with Ice Cream.

ELIZABETH'S ON 37TH'S MENU FOR SIX

Oyster Sausage Turnover With Apple Horseradish Sauce

Roasted Grouper With Sesame Almond Crust

Roast Zucchini

Ginger Poached Peaches

Oyster Sausage Turnover with Apple Horseradish Sauce

I n a large skillet over high heat, sauté the sausage and onion, stirring to break up the sausage. When the sausage is lightly browned, add the oysters, stir once and immediately spoon the mixture into a sieve and drain well. Discard the fat. Place in a bowl and toss in the cheeses. Cool and divide into 6 portions.

Place the 6 pastry circles on a buttered baking sheet and spoon oyster-sausage mixture into the center of each pastry circle. Fold each circle in half and crimp the edges with a fork to close.

Bake 10 minutes at 425° or until golden and crisp. Serve with Apple Horseradish Sauce.

© *Savannah Seasons*
Serves 6
Preparation Time:
  40 Minutes
Preheat oven to 425°

  1 **lb. spicy bulk Italian-style sausage**
  1 **cup onion, peeled, minced**
  1 **pint oysters, drained well; save juice for other recipes**
  1/3 **cup sharp cheddar cheese, grated**
  1/3 **cup mozzarella cheese, grated**
  1 **package puff pastry, cut into 6 circles the size of a coffee saucer**
  1/2 **cup Apple Horseradish Sauce (recipe follows)**

Apple Horseradish Sauce

© Savannah Seasons
Yield:
  1½ cups
Preparation Time:
  10 Minutes

  1 **cup sour cream or**
     yogurt
  2 **Tbsps. mayonnaise**
  1 **Tbsp. horseradish**
  1 **Granny Smith apple,**
     peeled, grated
  2 **Tbsps. fresh chives,**
     minced
  2 **Tbsps. fresh oregano or**
     Italian parsley, minced
     Dash of cayenne
     pepper

n a large mixing bowl whisk all ingredients together.

☆

Roasted Grouper
with Sesame Almond Crust

I n a medium-sized bowl, combine the sesame oil, vegetable oil, lemon juice, water, beaten egg, salt, pepper and chili sauce. Set aside.

Combine the wheat thins, cheese, almonds, sesame seeds, parsley, tarragon and pepper in the bowl of the food processor and process to crumbs. Put on a plate.

Dip the fish filets in the marinade, then in the crumbs. Place on a buttered shallow baking pan. Do not allow the filets to touch each other. Combine the butter and olive oil and drizzle over the fish, then roast in the oven for 20 minutes until browned and cooked through. Serve with peanut cream sauce.

Peanut Cream Sauce:

    2 cups peanut butter
    ¼ cup soy sauce
    4 tsps. hot chili sauce
    ½ cup lemon juice
    ¼ cup garlic
    1 cup water

Blend in the food processor.

© Savannah Seasons
Serves 6
Preparation Time:
** 45 Minutes**
Preheat oven to 425°

    2 Tbsps. sesame oil
    2 Tbsps. vegetable oil
    2 Tbsps. lemon juice
    2 Tbsps. water
    1 egg, beaten
    ¼ tsp. salt
    ¼ tsp. pepper
    1 tsp. hot chili sauce
    1 cup Stoned Wheat
      Thins or other crisp
      wheat crackers,
      crushed
    ½ cup Asiago cheese,
      grated
    ¼ cup almonds, toasted
    2 Tbsps. sesame seeds,
      toasted
    ¼ cup Italian parsley,
      minced
    2 Tbsps. tarragon,
      minced
    ½ tsp. cracked black
      pepper
    6 black grouper filets,
      6 oz., boneless,
      skinless, ½-inch thick
    2 Tbsps. butter, melted
    2 Tbsps. extra-virgin
      olive oil

☆

Roast Zucchini

© *Savannah Seasons*
Serves 6
Preparation Time:
  15 Minutes
Preheat oven to 400°

  3 **medium zucchini**
  ½ **cup melted butter**
  ¼ **cup fresh basil, minced**
  1 **Tbsp. fresh cracked**
    pepper
  ½ **cup Parmesan cheese,**
    grated

Scrub the zucchini well and cut into 1-inch-thick circles, discarding the ends. Place the circles side by side on a buttered baking sheet and lightly brush with melted butter. Sprinkle with basil and pepper and then with the grated cheese. Bake for 5 minutes in a 400° oven until crisp-tender and golden.

Ginger Poached Peaches

I n a large, non-reactive skillet, combine the sugar, ginger, allspice, lemon juice and grenadine. Over medium heat, bring to a boil while stirring. Add the peaches and bring back to a boil, stirring constantly, then lower the heat and simmer 5 minutes, until the peaches are soft, stirring occasionally. Turn off the heat and allow the peaches to cool in the liquid. Discard the 2 allspice seeds before serving.

Serve in individual glass bowls, topped with a dollop of orange sherbet and a mint sprig.

© *Savannah Seasons*
Serves 6
Preparation Time:
 30 Minutes

¾ **cup sugar**
 1 **tsp. fresh ginger,**
   peeled, minced
 2 **allspice seeds**
 2 **Tbsps. lemon juice**
 2 **tsps. grenadine**
 8 **large, fresh ripe**
   peaches, peeled, diced
   into 1-inch cubes
 1 **pint orange sherbet**
 6 **mint sprigs, garnish**

IL PASTICCIO

Il Pasticcio
ITALIAN CUISINE
2 East Broughton Street
Savannah, Georgia
(912) 231-8888
Dinner Daily 5PM–9:30PM
AVERAGE DINNER FOR TWO: $65

When asked where to find Il Pasticcio, Savannahians answer, "Follow the scents of garlic and roasting meats." The dining room is open, spacious and filled with diners enjoying a good Italian meal. The restaurant earns its name which means, "joyful chaos."

With an open kitchen concept of a wood-burning pizza oven and rotisserie, the menu at Il Pasticcio is loaded with roasted entrees. Many diners can't make up their minds as to what to order: Don't worry, Il Pasticcio offers a large selection of shared entrees that let diners sample many flavorful dishes.

Entrees that are "must tries" include a delicious house-made Minestrone, a handmade Rabbit Gnocchi with Fresh Herbs and Brown Butter, Grilled Shrimp with Fennel and Spicy Chile Sauce and a Crisped Lemon and Garlic Chicken with Mustard Mashed Potatoes.

IL PASTICCIO'S MENU FOR FOUR

Seafood Risotto

Seafood Risotto

Preheat a sauté pan and add the olive oil. Sauté the shrimp, fish and mussels. Cook until the shrimp turns bright red. Add the tomatoes, garlic and shallots. Remove the mussels and reserve them for garnish.

Deglaze the sauté pan with the wine. Add the cooked risotto and shrimp stock, stirring with a wooden spoon. Season with salt, pepper and fresh basil. Once the risotto has absorbed all the liquid, add the butter and Parmesan cheese.

Spoon the risotto into individual serving bowls, garnishing each bowl with 5 mussels and chopped parsley.

Serves 4
Preparation Time:
  1 Hour

  4 Tbsps. olive oil
  8 shrimp, peeled, deveined
  1 lb. firm white fish, cut into 4-inch pieces
 20 small mussels, well scrubbed
 ½ cup tomatoes, peeled, seeded, chopped
  1 tsp. garlic, chopped fine
  2 tsps. shallots, chopped fine
  2 cups Pinot Grigio
  4 cups risotto, cooked
  1 cup shrimp stock or clam broth
    Salt and pepper to taste
  2 tsps. fresh basil, sliced thin
  4 Tbsps. unsalted butter
  4 Tbsps. Parmesan cheese, shredded
  1 tsp. parsley, chopped

★

MRS. WILKES' BOARDING HOUSE

Mrs. Wilkes Boarding House
SOUTHERN CUISINE
107 West Jones Street
Savannah, Georgia
(912) 232-5997
Lunch 11AM–3PM
Dinner 5PM
AVERAGE DINNER FOR TWO: $20

Voted one of the 50 most distinguished restaurants in the United States by Conde Nast Traveler, Mrs. Wilkes Boarding House serves good, old-fashioned Southern cooking.

For more than 40 years, Mrs. Wilkes, the "Julia Child of country cooking," has been reigning over every meal served. In a flowery apron, she positions herself in the main dining room of the 1870 house as guests fill up the large, community tables. When all 60 places are taken, she instructs her daughter, granddaughter, son-in-law, grandson-in-law and a host of grandchildren to bring on the food. Guests are amazed at the big platters of crispy fried chicken, airy biscuits, huge squares of cornbread, pickled beets, candied yams and pitchers of sweet iced tea that are placed on the white oilcloth.

No one touches a morsel until Mrs. Wilkes says so. She rings a little bell…"Good Lord, bless this food to us," she prays. "And us to thy service. Amen." You can hear a pin drop. Then, bedlam.

Her self-published, spiral-bound cookbook, "Famous Recipes from Mrs. Wilkes' Boarding House in Historic Savannah" (150,000 copies in print), is stacked near the register, already autographed.

MRS. WILKES' BOARDING HOUSE'S MENU FOR FOUR

Chicken and Dumplings

Red Rice

Sour Cream Pound Cake

Chicken and Dumplings

P lace the chicken in a saucepan and cover with water. Add salt and pepper. Boil over medium heat for 30 minutes. Remove the chicken and save the broth to cook the dumplings.

For the dumplings: in a large mixing bowl, combine the flour, ½ cup of milk and the water and knead until the dough is firm. Mash flat on floured surface. Let stand about 10 minutes.

Roll dough out with rolling pin until knife-blade thin. Cut into 2-inch squares. Drop into boiling broth. Cook about 10 minutes on high heat. Reduce heat to low and return chicken to pot. Pour the remaining 1½ cups milk into the mixture and stir. Remove from heat. Season to taste.

© Famous Recipes from
Mrs. Wilkes' Boarding House
Serves 4
Preparation Time:
1 Hour

2½ **lbs. chicken, disjointed**
Water to cover
1 **tsp. salt**
1 **tsp. pepper**
2 **cups all-purpose flour**
2 **cups milk**
½ **cup water**

Red Rice

© *Famous Recipes from*
   Mrs. Wilkes' Boarding House
Serves 4
Preparation Time:
   45 Minutes
Preheat oven to 325°

   4 **bacon strips**
   2 **medium onions**
   2 **medium bell peppers**
   1 **can tomatoes**
   1 **can tomato sauce**
   ½ **tsp. Tabasco sauce**
   2 **cups rice, cooked**
      Salt and pepper to
      taste
   1 **tsp. Parmesan cheese**

ry bacon till crispy. Remove from pan and drain on paper towel. Brown the onions and bell peppers in the bacon drippings.

Add the tomatoes, tomato sauce, Tabasco and crumbled bacon.

Add the cooked rice and season to taste.

Pour into a greased casserole and sprinkle top with Parmesan cheese. Bake at 325° for 30 minutes or until rice is dry enough to separate.

Cooking Secret: For variation, try adding 1 lb. of cooked, deveined shrimp or 1 cup cooked sausage, pork or ham for a heartier meal.

Sour Cream Pound Cake

Cream the butter and sugar together in a large mixing bowl. Add egg yolks, one at a time, beating after each addition. Add the sour cream, then the sifted dry ingredients, mixing after each. Add flavorings.

Beat egg whites until stiff and fold into cake mixture.

Bake in a large tube or bundt pan at 325° for about 1 hour or until a toothpick comes out clean. Turn out of pan and allow to cool.

© *Famous Recipes from*
Mrs. Wilkes' Boarding House
Yield:
   1 bundt cake
Preparation Time:
   1½ Hours
Preheat oven to 325°

   1 cup butter
   3 cups sugar
   6 eggs, separated
   1 cup sour cream
   ¼ tsp. soda
   ¼ tsp. salt
   3 cups cake flour
   1 tsp. lemon flavoring
   1 tsp. vanilla flavoring

☆

THE PIRATE'S HOUSE

The Pirate's House
SEAFOOD CUISINE
20 East Broad Street
Savannah, Georgia
(912) 233-5757
Lunch 11:30AM–2:30PM
Dinner 5:30PM–9:45PM
AVERAGE DINNER FOR TWO: $45

Since about 1753, The Pirate's House has been welcoming visitors to Savannah with a bounty of delicious food and drink and rousing good times. Situated a short block from the Savannah River, The Pirate's House first opened as an inn for seafarers, and fast became a rendezvous for blood-thirsty pirates and sailors from the Seven Seas.

The history of those exciting days still hangs in the air. In the chamber known as the Captain's Rooms, with its hand-hewn ceiling beams joined with wooden pegs, diners have enjoyed extraordinary dishes for more than 30 years. The Pirate's House rambles in all different directions—each with a distinct charm all its own. Hanging on the wall are frames containing pages from an early and very rare edition of Robert Louis Stevenson's "Treasure Island." In fact, some of the action is supposed to have take place in The Pirate's House.

The validity of The Pirate's House has been recognized by the American Museum Society, which lists this historic tavern as a house museum. Today it is a mecca for Savannahians and tourists alike, who come to enjoy its many delicious Southern specialties served in the original setting of yesteryear.

THE PIRATE'S HOUSE MENU FOR FOUR

Okra Gumbo

Cranberry-Orange-Pecan Mold

Shrimp Creole

Cornbread

Key Lime Pie

Okra Gumbo

 ombine all the ingredients except the okra in a soup pot. Bring to a boil, lower heat and simmer for 1 hour. Add the okra and simmer for another 20 minutes.

Serves 6
Preparation Time:
  1½ Hours

  2 cans tomatoes,
    coarsely chopped,
    about 1 lb.
  1 Tbsp. tomato paste
  1 medium onion,
    coarsely chopped
  1 small bell pepper,
    coarsely chopped
 ⅓ cup ham, diced
  5 cups water
  1 tsp. salt
 ½ tsp. pepper
 ¾ tsp. Angostura bitters,
    optional
  1 lb. sliced okra

☆

Cranberry-Orange-Pecan Mold

Serves 6
Preparation Time:
15 Minutes
(note refrigeration time)

1 lb. cranberries
1 small orange, peeled,
  cut into 8 pieces
2 celery ribs, cut into
  2-inch lengths
1 cup sugar
½ cup pecans
1 box lemon or
  strawberry gelatin
2 cups boiling water

 hop the cranberries, orange and celery in a food processor. You may need to do it in 2 batches. Add the sugar and nuts and chop until fine but not mushy.

Dissolve the lemon or strawberry gelatin in boiling water. Stir the gelatin in a bowl over ice until slightly thickened. Stir the cranberry mixture into gelatin and pour into a well-oiled 5½- to 6-cup mold.

Refrigerate until set. Unmold and serve.

Shrimp Creole

Fry the bacon in a heavy pot. Add the onion, garlic, celery and bell pepper and cook until the onion is translucent. Add the remaining ingredients except the shrimp. Bring to a boil, lower heat and simmer uncovered, stirring occasionally until the sauce has thickened, about 30 to 40 minutes.

When sauce has reached desired thickness, add the shrimp and simmer until just cooked, about 5 minutes. Do not overcook shrimp.

Serve on white rice.

Serves 6
Preparation Time:
  1 Hour

¼ lb. bacon, chopped
1 medium onion,
    chopped
1 garlic clove, crushed
3 ribs celery, chopped
1 bell pepper, chopped
1 8 oz. bottle clam juice
1 cup chicken broth
1 small can tomato
    purée
1 Tbsp. fresh parsley,
    finely chopped
1 Tbsp. fresh chives
1 bay leaf
1 tsp. brown sugar
½ tsp. black pepper
1 tsp. Tabasco
1 tsp. lemon juice
    Dash of Worcestershire
    sauce
1 to 2 lbs. raw shrimp

Cornbread

Yield:
  1 8×8-inch pan
Preparation Time:
  50 Minutes
Preheat oven to 425°

1½ cups self-rising
    cornmeal
  1 cup self-rising flour
  1 tsp. baking powder
  ⅓ cup sugar
  1 cup milk
  1 cup half and half
  2 eggs
  ½ cup margarine, melted

Grease an 8×8-inch pan and place in the 425° oven.
    Combine the dry ingredients in a mixing bowl. Whisk in the milk, half and half, eggs and melted margarine. The batter should be a little thicker than heavy cream. If it is too thick, add more milk.

Remove the hot pan from the oven and pour in the batter. Return the pan to the oven and bake at 425° for 20 minutes, then lower heat to 350° and bake until a knife inserted in the center comes out clean, or about another 15 to 20 minutes.

Cut into squares and serve hot.

Cooking Secret: This recipe makes a lot of cornbread. You can easily cut the recipe in half. Bake in an 8×8-inch pan at 425° for 25 to 30 minutes or until golden brown. Your squares will be thinner, but just as tasty. Or bake a full recipe in a 9×13-inch pan for thinner squares.

☆

Key Lime Pie

Whisk the egg yolks, condensed milk, rind and juice together until smooth. Pour into the pie crust. Bake for 7 to 8 minutes at 375°. Cool on a wire rack for 15 minutes, then refrigerate until cold, at least 2 hours.

Spread the top with whipped cream and serve.

Cooking Secret: Ideally, you would use key limes, but they are hard to find. Thin skinned Florida limes are the next-best-thing, but any fresh limes are good.

Serves 8
Preparation Time:
  30 Minutes
(note refrigeration time)
Preheat oven to 375°

  3 **egg yolks**
  1 **can sweetened**
    condensed milk, 15 oz.
    Rind of 1 lime, grated
$\frac{1}{2}$ **cup fresh lime juice**
  1 **graham cracker crust,**
    9-inch
  1 **cup heavy cream,**
    whipped, sweetened
    to taste

THE CLOISTER

The Cloister
Sea Island, Georgia 31561
(800) SEA ISLAND
(912) 638-3611
ROOM RATES: $124–$712

T his enchanting Mobil 5-Star, world-renowned resort is located on a narrow, well-forested sliver of southeast Georgia real estate, offering miles of private beach for its guests. Between Sea Island and adjacent St. Simons Island, some 10,000 acres of nature wait to be discovered in the forests and marshes beside the Atlantic.

More than 250 guest rooms, clustered at the southern shore of the island, are located in the Main Building, River House, Guest Houses and Beach Houses. The Cloister operates on the full American Plan—all meals are included.

Much of the Cloister's landscape is devoted to its premier golf course, sparkling with blooming plantings. There is something for every person and every lifestyle, including 18 superb tennis courses, horseback rides on the beach, sail-boarding, fishing charters, swimming, biking, lawn sports and yes, even ballroom dancing.

At the Sea Island Spa, professionally directed fitness and spa services are offered at state-of-the-art facilities. Spa packages include massage, reflexology, facials, nutrition and fitness consultation, personal training sessions and Hungarian Kur Baths.

Peach Soup

I n a stainless steel pot, combine the peaches, brown sugar, cinnamon and water. Over low heat, cook until the peaches start to soften. Remove from heat and allow to cool.

Add the lemon juice and schnapps. Place peach mixture in a blender and purée. Taste and adjust seasoning if desired. Cover and chill before serving.

Serves 4
Preparation Time:
  15 Minutes
(note refrigeration time)

5 large ripe peaches
   peeled, seeded
1 cup brown sugar
   Cinnamon to taste
1 qt. water
   Lemon juice to taste
1 oz. peach schnapps

FORSYTH PARK INN

Forsyth Park Inn
102 West Hall Street
Savannah, Georgia 31401-5562
(912) 233-6800
ROOM RATES: $90–$175, continental breakfast included

The Forsyth Park Inn is an 1890 Queen Ann Victorian sea captains' mansion, elegantly restored to create the pampered lifestyle of the 19th century. Exuding warm and friendly "Southern charm," the large rooms feature period furnishings with four-poster king- and queen-sized beds, unique fireplaces, antique marble baths or whirlpool tubs and carefully preserved architectural details such as 16-foot ceilings and 14-foot carved oak doors with a grand staircase. A private carriage cottage nestled in the courtyard is also available for romantic getaways.

Located in Savannah's National Historic District, the inn overlooks Forsyth Park, Savannah's largest and most opulent park, filled with moss-laden oaks, blooming azaleas, scented magnolias, lighted monuments and a sparkling fountain.

Early evenings begin with refreshments and wine in the parlor. Continental breakfast is offered by the widely traveled mother-and-son innkeepers.

Tropical Muffins

Combine the bran, flour, baking soda, salt, raisins and coconut and mix.

In a separate bowl, beat together the eggs. Add the butter, milk, oil, banana and honey. Add the wet mixture to the dry ingredients. Mix until well blended.

Fill greased or paper-lined muffin pans ½ to ⅔ full. Bake at 375° for approximately 20 minutes or until lightly browned.

Yields 18 to 30 Muffins
Preparation Time:
  40 Minutes
Preheat oven to 375°

2½ cups unprocessed bran
1⅓ cups all-purpose or
   whole wheat flour
2½ tsps. baking soda
 ½ tsp. salt
  1 cup raisins
  1 cup coconut, shredded
   or flaked
  2 eggs
 ½ cup buttermilk
 ½ cup vegetable oil
  1 cup ripe banana,
   mashed
 ½ cup honey

★

GREYFIELD INN

Greyfield Inn
Cumberland Island, Georgia
Mailing Address: P.O. Box 900
Fernandino Beach, Florida 32035-0900
(904) 261-6408
ROOM RATES: $295–$350

L ocated on Cumberland Island, the inn was built in 1901 as a wedding gift from Thomas and Lucy Carnegie to their daughter, Margaret. A stay at the Greyfield Inn is a step back in time—a place to relax, unwind and take a breather from the hustle and bustle of everyday life.

The inn consists of 13 guest rooms—nine in the main house and four cottage rooms. Bathrooms in the main house are shared. Under the supervision of two chefs, the inn provides three meals a day for guests.

Eighty percent of Cumberland Island is owned by the National Park Service and is a National Seashore. The park service provides the only other accommodations, and they are campsites. Cumberland is a primitive island without paved roads, shops or street lights. What it does have are wild horses, deer, armadillos, hogs and other wildlife roaming free. Guests are encouraged to make use of the bicycles provided by the inn to explore the island. Greyfield Inn provides a tour with a naturalist.

Cranberry-Raisin Scones

I n a large bowl, combine the flour, salt, sugar and baking powder. Add cranberries and raisins. With a wooden spoon, stir in cream and mix until dough holds together.

Knead dough 5 to 10 times or until the dough is easily handled but still moist. Put onto floured board. Roll out to ¼-inch thick or just a bit more. Cut into 3-inch diamonds. Brush with melted butter and sprinkle with sugar.

Place scones 1 inch apart on cookie sheet and bake at 400° for 12 to 15 minutes.

Yield:
  24 scones
Preparation Time:
  30 Minutes
Preheat oven to 400°

  4 cups all-purpose flour
  1 tsp. salt
  ½ cup sugar
  1 Tbsp. baking powder
  1 cup dried cranberries
  ½ cup golden raisins
  2½ cups heavy cream

☆

JEKYLL ISLAND CLUB HOTEL

Jekyll Island Club Hotel
371 Riverview Drive
Jekyll Island, Georgia 31527
(800) 535-9547
(912) 635-2600
ROOM RATES: $49–$510

F ounded in 1886 as an exclusive hunting retreat for the very rich, Jekyll Island Club Hotel invites guests to experience all the splendor and charm once reserved for the Morgans, Rockefellers and Vanderbilts. A short walk from the oceanfront, millionaires arrived aboard their yachts to enjoy the "season."

This Victorian treasure, recognized as a National Historic Landmark and restored for future generations, is a unique resort with architectural character and a charming historic ambiance. The driveway curves to the front of the hotel with a croquet lawn on the right and a poolside garden on the left.

The Queen Ann architecture of the hotel is distinguishable by the turret on the roof, bay windows and verandas. The rooms have views of the gardens, intracoastal waterways and vast marshlands. The hotel's amenities include a heated swimming pool, indoor/outdoor tennis, basketball, croquet, putting green, bike rentals, 63 holes of championship golf, deep-sea fishing, jogging trails, horseback riding, health club, cable water skiing and horse-drawn carriage rides.

Baked Brie en Croute with Brown Sugar and Almonds

L ay out pastry dough and brush with 1 tsp. of the egg yolk. Place a layer of brown sugar about the size of the brie round on the sheet dough. Add the almond slices. Place the brie round on top of the almonds.

Add sugar to the top of brie round and top with more almonds. Fold the dough around the brie and seal. Refrigerate at least 30 minutes.

Preheat oven to 450°. Brush the outside of pastry-covered brie with the remaining egg wash. Bake until golden brown, about 4 minutes.

Serve on a bed of brown sugar and almonds.

Serves 4
Preparation Time:
  40 Minutes
(note refrigeration time)
Preheat oven to 450°

1 **sheet puff pastry dough**
2 **egg yolks, beaten**
2 **cups brown sugar**
1 **round of brie**
1 **cup almond slices, toasted**

MULBERRY INN

Mulberry Inn
601 East Bay Street
Savannah, Georgia 31401
(912) 238-1200
ROOM RATES: $145–$185

Savannah is a treasure-trove of architectural history dating back to the Revolutionary and Civil Wars. Perched in the heart of the city's historic district on Washington Square is the award-winning Mulberry Inn.

Built in 1860 as a livery stable, the building served as a cotton warehouse in the late 1800s, as well as a Coca-Cola bottling plant in the early 1900s. After a period of vacancy, followed by extensive renovation, Mulberry opened in 1982 as a charming inn.

Guest rooms have been decorated to enhance the Old South character and charm of the hotel. The inn is garnished with period furnishings, oil paintings, polished hardwood floors and elegant chandeliers that offer guests a window into Savannah's gracious past.

The inn's Cafe, serving breakfast and lunch, overlooks the courtyard, while The Mulberry Room beckons guests for dinner. After dinner, enjoy cocktails at Sgt. Jasper's Lounge or unwind in the rooftop Jacuzzi, overlooking the Savannah River.

Southern Style Potatoes

Boil or steam the potatoes until tender yet firm. Cool in the refrigerator for 20 minutes.

In a large mixing bowl combine the mayonnaise, sour cream, relish, bell pepper, onion, dill, mustard and salt and pepper.

Add the potatoes.

Garnish with sweet paprika.

Serves 8
Preparation Time:
  45 Minutes

- 4 cups red skinned potatoes, medium diced
- ¾ cup mayonnaise
- ¼ cup sour cream
- ¼ cup dill pickle relish
- ½ bell pepper, medium diced
- 2 Tbsps. onion, finely diced
- 2 tsps. fresh dill, chopped
- 1 Tbsp. mustard
  Salt and pepper to taste
  Sweet paprika for garnish

LOUISIANA:
Mardi Gras
and a
Whole Lot More

Water, water everywhere—more than 7,500 miles of navigable waterways—the Mississippi, Ouachita and Red Rivers, giant lakes, such as Pontchartrain, great Bayous, (marshlands), all drain into the Gulf of Mexico. Louisiana is relatively flat. The highest point in the state, Driskill Mountain, is only 525 feet above sea level. Louisiana's culture is truly "different" from the rest of the nation—political subdivisions are measured by parishes rather than counties; while the rest of the country is based on British common law, the French Code Napoleon is the basis of law in Louisiana.

Although it all started with Spanish explorer Hernando de Soto, it was Robert Cavalier de La Salle who claimed the Louisiana territory for France in 1682. Twenty-five years later, the "real" history of Louisiana began with the founding of New Orleans. Louisiana Creoles, descendants of early French and/or Spanish settlers, were followed in 1755 by Acadians ("Cajuns"), French settlers in Nova Scotia, Canada, who were forcibly transferred by the British to Louisiana (an event commemorated in Longfellow's *Evangeline*). The Cajuns settled near Bayou Teche. Another group, the Islenos, Canary Islanders, were brought to Louisiana by a Spanish governor in 1770.

The next forty years were tumultuous indeed. Louisiana was a financial drain, so France ceded it to Spain in 1762; but when the expensive French and Indian War came to an end, Napoleon Bonaparte coerced Spain into giving it back in 1800. Only three years later, France needed money to fight yet another war against England, so it sold Louisiana to the young American government for $15 million. In 1812, Louisiana became the 18th state to enter the union, but in 1815, after the Treaty of Ghent had supposedly ended the War of 1812 between Britain and the United States, British forces invaded New Orleans. Andrew Jackson, with the help of Creoles, Choctaw Indians, slaves, pirates (including Jean Lafitte) and frontiersmen, soundly defeated the English, becoming a national hero and ultimately propelling himself into the White House.

From 1800 to 1860, Louisiana's population grew from 50,000 to 700,000, due to plantation agriculture. The Civil War, insects, poor weather and mechanization all but destroyed Louisiana's farm base. It was not until 1901, when the first oil well revealed the vast mineral resources of the State, that

Louisiana started to recover. But inept—or corrupt—politicians failed to tax profits and, as a result, the bounty of the petro-chemical industry went to northern corporations.

The years 1928 to 1935 marked the era of Huey "Kingfish" Long, the charismatic governor who was loved and vilified more than any other politician in the state's history. Although he exercised dictatorial power and corruption second to none, many said he would have been elected president of the United States had he not been felled by an assassin's bullet.

After World War II, petroleum and natural gas continued as Louisiana's greatest sources of wealth, but with the collapse of prices in the early 1980s, the state faced economic collapse and was saved only by a dramatic rise in tourism. Louisiana is the third-largest refiner of petroleum in the United States. It's rated among the top ten producers of sweet potatoes, sugar cane, rice, cotton, pecans and soybeans. More than a quarter of all seafood landed in the United States comes from Louisiana. New Orleans and Baton Rouge are among the five busiest ports in the United States. And then there's New Orleans—Dixieland, Bourbon Street and Mardi Gras...

Famous Louisianans include Louis Armstrong, Judah Philip Benjamin (Jewish treasurer of the Confederacy), Antoine "Fats" Domino, Pete Fountain, Al Hirt, Huey Long, Branford Marsalis, Winton Marsalis, Henry Miller and Paul Prudhomme.

Here are some of the highlights of a trip to Louisiana.

AVERY ISLAND, reached by a toll bridge, is underlaid by a great salt dome. The two primary attractions, one natural and one gastronomic, are the JUNGLE GARDENS, 200 acres of sub-tropical flora, sunken gardens, more than 20,000 herons, deer, alligators and a Chinese garden with a Buddha dating from 1,000 A.D., and the McIlhenny Company, which has been manufacturing Tabasco® brand red capsicum pepper sauce since 1868.

BATON ROUGE, Louisiana's capital, houses the STATE CAPITOL, constructed of marble from every marble-producing country in the world, and the LOUISIANA STATE UNIVERSITY RURAL LIFE MUSEUM, which re-creates an 1800s plantation.

CAJUN BAYOU COUNTRY is widespread. You can take Cajun swamp cruises in **HOUMA, KRAEMER, LAFAYETTE, JEAN LAFITTE, SLIDELL** and **WESTWEGO.** At Vermillion-ville, south of Lafayette, there's a 23-acre living history re- cre-

Louisiana Governor Huey P. Long

Photos from the Louisiana Department of State, Division of Archives, Records Management and History, John B. Gasquet Collection

The State Capitol in Baton Rouge

ation of 17th and 18th century Cajun and Creole Louisiana. To savor the true flavor of Cajun Country, a trip to **ST. MARTINVILLE** is a must. Legends of Evangeline, the character created by Longfellow, proliferate. The EVANGELINE OAK, at the foot of Port Street, where Evangeline and her lover are said to have met, is said to be the most photographed tree in America. The LONGFELLOW-EVANGELINE STATE COMMEMORATIVE

St. Louis Cathedral and Jackson Square in New Orleans. The inscription on the statue of Andrew Jackson reads, "The Union Must & Shall Be Preserved."

Photo from the Louisiana Department of State, Division of Archives, Records Management and History, John B. Gasquet Collection

AREA, a 157-acre preserve bordering Bayou Teche, houses a large plantation and exhibits depicting Cajun life in the mid-19th century. ST. MARTIN DE TOURS CATHOLIC CHURCH, established in 1765, features a baptismal font donated by King Louis XVI and the grave of Emmeline Labiche, thought to be the heroine of Longfellow's *Evangeline*.

All roads lead to "The Big Easy"— **NEW ORLEANS,** whose very contradictions only add to its charm. Elegant brick and plaster buildings with gilded iron balconies stand in the shadow of soaring skyscrapers. Ocean-going liners dock adjacent to vegetable vendors selling produce from mule-drawn wagons. Unquestionably the heart of the City—the magnet that draws millions of visitors each year—is *Vieux Carré*—the FRENCH QUARTER. Typical of New Orleans' contradictions, the "French Quarter" is actually Spanish! Disastrous fires destroyed most of the original French buildings.

Legendary characters of yesteryear haunt the district. On Bourbon Street, near upper-crust Royal Street, Jean and Pierre Lafitte operated a fencing operation for their pirate contraband. Voodoo queen Marie Laveau frequented St. Louis Cathedral. Maspero's Exchange on Chartres Street was for years a hotbed of political intrigue, with would-be "liberators" constantly plotting the overthrow of revolution-ripe banana republics to the South. There's the BEAUREGARD-KEYES HOUSE, home to Confederate General Beauregard; the CABILDO STATE HOUSE, from which the Spanish governor ruled; the HERMANN-GRIMA HOUSE, a restored 1831 mansion with Creole kitchen, slave

☆

quarters and Creole cooking demonstrations; and, at the very heart of the French Quarter, JACKSON SQUARE, the Quarter's unofficial Left Bank. ST. LOUIS CATHEDRAL is one of the oldest (1794) and most photographed churches in the country. If you're a Wax Museum buff, you'll love the MUSEE CONTI WAX MUSEUM, with historically accurate settings covering New Orleans' history from 1699 to the present.

If you don't stop in at PRESERVATION HALL, you may as well miss New Orleans altogether. Each night five or six bands take turns performing traditional jazz in its purest form. Expect to wait in line a long time, then stand through the entire performance. And expect to come out feeling it was well worth the wait and the discomfort!

New Orleans' dining and night life are legendary. The city is home to two authentic American cuisines—Cajun and Creole. Both come from French, Spanish and African kitchens. Creole originated in the French Quarter and Cajun cooking developed in the Bayou areas of the state. Cajun is traditionally hotter and heartier than Creole cuisine and is characterized by hot peppers, sausages and roux.

The city's reputation for nightlife began when the first women France sent to New Orelans quickly turned to the world's oldest profession. The raw frontier atmosphere welcomed them with open arms, as it were, and soon New Orleans was one of the pleasure capitals of the world. Storyville preached control rather than suppression. Today the "scandals" of another era are more nostalgic than actual, but watch yourself and your wallet on Bourbon Street, home of strip joints and sharks, where anything goes—including your money. Jazz was born in New Orleans and still forms the basis of The Big Easy's abundant nightlife, from Pete Fountain's Night Club in the New Orleans Hilton, to Preservation Hall.

The one event synonymous with New Orleans is MARDI GRAS. The actual Mardi Gras period is only the last third of Carnival Season (January 6 to Shrove Tuesday). In a sense, Mardi Gras lasts all year: the planning for next year's celebration begins just after Lent. There are parades, private balls and gaiety unmatched anywhere in the United States—the epitome of the Latin trait of total joyousness followed by total solemnity.

☆

ARNAUD'S

Arnaud's
CREOLE AND CONTINENTAL CUISINE
813 Bienville Street
New Orleans, Louisiana
(800) 453-1020
(504) 523-5433
Lunch Monday–Friday 11:30AM–2:30PM
Dinner Daily 6PM–10PM
AVERAGE DINNER FOR TWO: $85

I n 1918, Arnaud Cazenave opened the doors of Arnaud's and a legend began. Dubbed the "Count" by his friends, he spent thirty years building the restaurant into one of the finest dining establishments in the United States. Upon the "Count's" death, his daughter, Germaine Wells, took over the restaurant. Archie Casbarian, today's proprietor, was her hand-picked successor, and took over in 1978.

Archie and Jane Casbarian, award-winning restaurateurs, have taken Arnaud's tradition to new heights. The menu is a combination of French and Creole cookery featuring signature dishes such as Shrimp Arnaud, which is Gulf shrimp marinated in the famous tangy Creole Remoulade Sauce. Oyster Bienville is Arnaud's creation of shrimp and mushrooms in a White Wine Sauce. The Speckled Trout Meunière is a crispy fried filet of speckled trout served with a Creole Meunière Sauce. Arnaud's offers a variety of fish, fowl, veal, seafood and steaks on their menu.

In a city famous for great dining, music and festivity at all hours of the day and night, Sunday brunch and jazz are a great combination at Arnaud's with diners listening to a live New Orleans-style jazz band.

ARNAUD'S MENU FOR FOUR

Oysters Bienville

Watercress à la Germaine

Arnaud's Shrimp Creole

Stuffed Rock Cornish Game Hens with Bordelaise Sauce

Café Brûlot

Oysters Bienville

I n a large, heavy saucepan, sauté the chopped mushrooms quickly in the vegetable oil. Remove from pan and set aside.

In the same pan, melt the unsalted butter and sauté the garlic and shallots, stirring frequently until soft. Add the diced shrimp, then sprinkle in the flour. Stir all together, add the reserved mushrooms. Deglaze the pan with the brandy while stirring constantly. Stir in the heavy cream and cook until smooth. Add the Romano cheese, dry bread crumbs, parsley, salt, pepper and cayenne. A small amount of milk may be added if the mixture is too thick.

Remove from heat and allow to cool. Refrigerate for about 1½ hours.

Thirty minutes before you plan to bake the oysters, place the pans of rock salt in a preheated 500° oven.

Wash oyster shells well, pat dry. Place oysters on shells, putting six in each pan of rock salt. Spoon one heaping tablespoon of sauce over each oyster. Bake for 15 to 18 minutes until well browned.

Serves 4
Preparation Time:
   40 Minutes
(note refrigeration time)
Preheat oven to 500°

- ⅔ cup mushrooms, finely chopped
- 1 Tbsp. vegetable oil
- 4 Tbsps. unsalted butter
- 1½ tsps. garlic, finely minced
- 1 Tbsp. shallots, finely chopped
- ½ lb. boiled shrimp, finely diced
- 1 Tbsp. flour
- ½ cup brandy
- ½ cup heavy cream
- 6 Tbsps. Romano cheese, grated
- 4 Tbsps. dry bread crumbs
- ¼ cup parsley, finely minced
- 1 tsp. salt
- 1 tsp. ground white pepper
- ½ tsp. cayenne pepper
- Milk, optional
- 24 oysters on the half shell, drained
- 4 pans rock salt

Watercress à la Germaine

Serves 4
Preparation Time:
  15 Minutes

  3 bunches watercress,
    cleaned
  2 cups mushrooms,
    sliced
  ¾ cup watercress
    dressing (recipe
    follows)
  12 cherry tomatoes

Watercress Dressing:
  ½ cup mayonnaise
  ¼ cup sour cream
  ⅛ cup Creole cream
    cheese*
  1¼ tsps. green
    peppercorns, crushed
  2 Tbsps. green onions or
    scallions, chopped
  1¼ tsps. Worcestershire
    sauce
    Dash of Tabasco sauce
    Salt and white pepper
    to taste

D ivide the watercress among serving plates and top with the mushrooms. Drizzle the dressing over the salad and garnish each plate with cherry tomatoes.

Using a mixer at low speed, blend the mayonnaise, sour cream and cream cheese for 3 minutes. Add the crushed peppercorns, green onions, Worcestershire and Tabasco. Blend for another 3 minutes. Season to taste with salt and white pepper.

* Creole cream cheese, a single large curd surrounded by cream, is a unique New Orleans product. If it's not available in your area, a good substitute is heavy cream poured over either farmer cheese or large-curd cottage cheese.

Arnaud's Shrimp Creole

H eat the olive oil in a skillet over high heat. Add the shrimp and stir for a minute, until they are heated through. Add the Creole sauce and bring to a boil. Reduce the heat and simmer for 3 minutes. Season to taste with salt and pepper.

For the sauce: Heat the olive oil over high heat, then add the onion, green pepper, celery and parsley. Stir and cook for about 2 minutes, then add the garlic. Stir in the veal stock and chicken base or bouillon, add the bouquet garni, diced tomatoes and tomato purée and bring to a boil. Reduce the heat, allow to simmer for 10 minutes. Season to taste with the salt, pepper, Tabasco and cayenne.

To serve, divide the rice among dinner plates and spoon the shrimp and sauce over each serving. Sprinkle with chopped parsley. Serve at once.

* Bouquet garni is comprised of ½ bunch parsley, 3 bay leaves, 1 bunch fresh thyme and 1 stalk celery, tied together with butcher's twine. Leave a long tail of twine and tie the bouquet to the handle of the pot.

Serves 4
Preparation Time:
  30 Minutes

  4 Tbsps. virgin olive oil
  3 lbs. boiled shrimp
  3 cups Creole Sauce
     (recipe follows)
     Salt and freshly
     ground black pepper
     to taste
4½ cups white rice,
     cooked
  ½ cup fresh parsley,
     chopped

Creole Sauce:
  2 Tbsps. olive oil
  1 cup white onion,
     chopped
  ½ cup green pepper,
     diced
1½ cups celery, chopped
  ½ cup fresh parsley,
     chopped
  1 garlic clove, chopped
  2 cups veal stock
1¼ tsps. chicken base or
     bouillon
  1 bouquet garni*
  ½ cup diced tomatoes
1½ cups tomato purée
     Salt and freshly
     ground pepper to taste
     Tabasco to taste
     Cayenne pepper to
     taste

Stuffed Rock Cornish Game Hens with Bordelaise Sauce

Serves 4
Preparation Time:
 1½ Hours
Preheat oven to 400°

Stuffing:
 4 Tbsps. shallots,
  chopped
 ¾ cup ruby port
 2 large eggs
 ¼ cup heavy cream
 1 Tbsp. parsley, chopped
 ¼ cup pork tenderloin,
  finely minced
 1 cup veal top round,
  finely minced
 2 Tbsps. fat back, finely
  minced
 ½ tsp. crushed thyme
  Salt and freshly
  ground pepper to taste

**Stuffed Rock Cornish
Game Hens:**
 4 Cornish game hens
  Salt and freshly
  ground black pepper
  to taste
 4 slices bacon
 1 qt. veal stock

Stuffing:
In a large mixing bowl, combine all the ingredients and mix to a smooth, mousse-like consistency. Refrigerate until ready to use.

Stuffed Rock Cornish Game Hens:
Divide stuffing among the four game hens, which have been seasoned with salt and pepper. Wrap each stuffed bird in a slice of bacon. Place in a roasting pan. Pour veal stock over, cover and braise in the oven for about 45 minutes. When done, remove hens to a warm platter, discarding the bacon.

☆

Sauce Enhancements:

In a saucepan, sauté the mushrooms quickly in clarified butter. Then add the chopped tomatoes and Bordelaise Sauce (recipe follows). Heat through and adjust the seasonings, adding chopped parsley.

To serve, pour sauce over hens on a large serving platter. Garnish with cherry tomatoes and parsley sprigs. Serve immediately.

Cooking Secret: To save time make the stuffing in advance and refrigerate. The Bordelaise Sauce may also be made a bit ahead.

Sauce Enhancements:

1 cup mushrooms, quartered

4 Tbsps. clarified butter

2 whole tomatoes, peeled, chopped
  Bordelaise Sauce (recipe follows)
  Salt and white pepper to taste

1 Tbsp. parsley, chopped
  Cherry tomatoes for garnish
  Parsley sprigs for garnish

Bordelaise Sauce

Preparation Time:
  20 Minutes

  2 **Tbsps. butter**
  ¼ **cup shallots, chopped**
  1 **cup red wine**
  1 **bouquet garni***
  1 **whole clove**
  1 **black peppercorn**
  1 **bay leaf**
  ½ **garlic clove**
  1 **qt. veal stock**
  1 **Tbsp. glacé de viande†**
     Salt and freshly
     ground pepper to taste

Melt the butter in a pan over high heat, then add the shallots and cook until translucent. Add the red wine and bring to a boil, then add the bouquet garni, clove, peppercorn, bay leaf, garlic and veal stock. Reduce heat and simmer until the volume is reduced by half and coats a spoon. Stir in the glacé de viande. Strain, then season to taste with salt and pepper.

* Bouquet garni is ½ bunch parsley, 3 bay leaves, 1 bunch fresh thyme and 1 stalk celery, tied together with butcher's twine. Leave a long tail of twine and tie the bouquet to the handle of the pot.

† Glacé de viande is French for "meat glaze," made by boiling meat juices until they are reduced to a thick syrup. It is used to add flavor and color to sauces.

☆

Café Brûlot

Combine the cinnamon, cloves, fruit peel and sugar lumps over heat in a brûlot bowl or chafing dish and crush them together, using the back of the ladle. Add the brandy and Curaçao and mix well. When the mixture begins to boil, ignite and keep stirring to dissolve the sugar. Add the black coffee very gradually. Ladle into special brûlot demitasse cups.

The traditional brûlot ladle has a strainer to catch the spices. When using an ordinary ladle, be careful to fill it with only the liquid.

Serve the Café Brûlot as a delightful dessert on its own or with a dessert. Café Brûlot is a festive addition to a special dinner or any occasion.

Serves 4
Preparation Time:
  10 Minutes

- 1 **cinnamon stick**
- 6 **whole cloves**
- ¼ **cup orange peel, slivered**
- ¼ **cup lemon peel, slivered**
- 3 **lumps sugar**
- ½ **cup brandy**
- 2 **Tbsps. Curaçao (orange liqueur)**
- 3 **cups hot, strong black coffee**

☆

BELLA LUNA

Bella Luna
CONTINENTAL AND SOUTHWESTERN CUISINE
914 North Peters Street
New Orleans, Louisiana
(504) 529-1583
Dinner Monday–Saturday 6PM–10:30PM
Dinner Sunday 6PM–9:30PM
AVERAGE DINNER FOR TWO: $75

T he moon…the stars…the river. Wonderful surroundings and great, great food. Bella Luna is located in the French Quarter, where Dumaine meets the river.

The eclectic menu has gained rave reviews, both from the critics and knowledgeable New Orleans restaurant-goers. Too varied to be easily pigeon-holed, the menu appetizingly blends New Orleans, Continental and even Southwestern specialties.

Menu highlights include Freshly Steamed Maine Lobster Tossed with Calamari-Ink Colored Fettuccine; Roma Tomatoes, Fresh Basil and Saffron Aioli; Sautéed Redfish in a Sweet Basil Pesto Crust Served with Wilted Spinach; a Tasso Stuffed Shrimp with Persimmon Habañero Salsa and Homegrown Cilantro; and Oven Roasted Quail Stuffed with Crawfish and Crabmeat over a White Chocolate Tomatillo Salsa. The extensive wine menu includes selections from California, France and Italy.

BELLA LUNA'S MENU FOR FOUR

Creole Crab Cakes with Pico de Gallo

Lobster Medallions with Vanilla Vinaigrette

Baked Snapper with Grilled Pineapple

Pecan Breaded Pork Chops with Beer Sauce

Mint Chocolate Ice Soufflé

Creole Crab Cakes with Pico de Gallo

Sauté the celery and onion in a hot skillet with a little olive oil or butter and then let them cool. After cubing the French bread, mix the remaining ingredients together (keep a little of the bread crumbs aside to coast hands when forming the cakes).

Form the crab cakes to the desired size, and sauté them in the skillet with olive oil for 2 to 3 minutes on each side.

For the pico de gallo: Mix all ingredients together in a large mixing bowl. Let set for 1 hour. Re-season to taste.

Serves 4
Preparation Time:
 40 Minutes
(note refrigeration time)

  2 celery stalks, finely
    diced
  1 large onion, finely
    diced
    Olive oil
  4 cups French bread,
    ¼-inch cubes
  1 lb. crab meat, shelled
  ½ red bell pepper, finely
    diced
  ½ green bell pepper,
    finely diced
  2 Tbsps. dry mustard
  1 tsp. cayenne pepper
  1 Tbsp. garlic powder
  1 Tbsp. onion powder
  3 egg whites
  2 cups bread crumbs
  ½ cup mayonnaise

Pico de Gallo:
  1 bunch cilantro, finely
    chopped
  1 large red onion, finely
    chopped
  3 serrano chile peppers,
    finely chopped
  1 lb. tomatoes, diced
    Juice of 3 limes
    Cumin to taste
    Salt and pepper to
    taste

★

Lobster Medallions with Vanilla Vinaigrette

Serves 4
Preparation Time:
  15 Minutes
(note refrigeration time)

  1 **vanilla bean**
  ¼ **cup sherry vinegar**
  ½ **cup grape seed oil**
     Salt, pepper and sugar
     to taste
  2 **shallots, finely diced**
  ½ **cup arugula**
  ½ **red onion, sliced**
  1 **tomato, sliced**
  1 **avocado, sliced**
  1 **lobster, steamed, about**
     1½ lbs.
     Pinch of chervil

Cut the vanilla bean in half the long way and scrape out the seeds. Mix the seeds with the vinegar and oil and season with salt, pepper and sugar. Add the shallots and let the vinaigrette sit for 4 hours to intensify the vanilla flavor.

Arrange the arugula, onions, tomatoes and avocados on a plate. Place the lobster medallion and claw on top. Drizzle the vinaigrette over the lobster and salad. Garnish with fresh chervil flakes.

☆

Baked Snapper with Grilled Pineapple

Season the snapper with juice from 1 lemon, salt, pepper and Worcestershire. Let rest for 10 minutes, then remove from liquid. Sprinkle with thyme and rosemary.

In a sauté pan, melt ½ stick of butter over medium heat until golden brown. Add the snapper and sauté for 2 minutes on each side. Finish in the oven at 375° for 10 to 12 minutes.

Sauté the shallots in 1 Tbsp. butter, then add the vermouth, cream and orange juice. Reduce until ⅓ of the liquid remains, then add pink peppercorns and whisk in the remaining butter. Remove from the heat until ready to use. Do not let it cool down completely. Immediately before serving add the finely chopped basil.

Clean the pineapples and cut in half from the top to the bottom, then cut in to ¼-inch-thick slices.

Mix together the rice wine vinegar, mint and garlic and marinate the pineapple slices for a few minutes. Remove from the liquid, then season with salt and pepper and grill on both sides with olive oil long enough to create grill marks. The pineapple can now be placed on the dinner plate.

On the plate, place the grilled pineapple, topped with the snapper and lightly cover with the citrus peppercorn sauce. Garnish with fresh basil and the remaining lemons, cut in quarters.

Serves 6
Preparation Time:
   45 Minutes
Preheat oven to 375°

- 6 snapper filets, 6 to 8 oz. each
- 4 whole lemons
  Salt and pepper to taste
- 3 Tbsps. Worcestershire sauce
- 2 Tbsps. lemon thyme, chopped
- 1 Tbsp. rosemary, chopped
- 1 stick butter
- 3 shallots, finely chopped
- ¼ cup vermouth
- ¼ cup whipping cream
  Juice from 20 oranges
- 3 Tbsps. pink peppercorns
- 2 Tbsps. basil, finely chopped
- 2 fresh ripe pineapples
- ¼ cup seasoned rice wine vinegar
- 2 Tbsps. mint, chopped
- 1 tsp. garlic, chopped
- 2 tsps. olive oil

☆

Pecan Breaded Pork Chops with Beer Sauce

Serves 6
Preparation Time:
 30 Minutes
Preheat oven to 350°

 1 cup pecans
 1 cup bread crumbs
 1 tsp. dry mustard
 1 tsp. celery salt
   Salt and pepper to
   taste
 6 pork chops
 1 cup flour
 1 egg, beaten
 4 Tbsps. butter

Beer Sauce:
 1 cup onions
 1 tsp. garlic
 1 Tbsp. caraway seeds
 1 bottle beer
 2 cups demi-glace
   Salt and pepper to
   taste

Mix together the pecans, bread crumbs and seasonings in a food processor. Dust the pork chops with flour, then dip in egg wash. Bread with the pecan mixture. Sauté the pork chops in butter on both sides until brown, then bake in a 350° oven for 15 minutes until fully cooked.

Beer Sauce:
Sauté the onions, garlic and caraway seeds over medium heat. Deglaze with the beer and demi-glace and cook for 15 minutes. Finish with salt and pepper to taste. Pour over top of hot pecan-breaded pork chops.

☆

Mint Chocolate Ice Soufflé

Whisk together the egg yolks, eggs and powdered sugar over a double boiler. Then sit it on a bed of ice and whisk until it is cooled. After the mixture is cool, add the schnapps, mint and chocolate. Then fold in the whipped cream.

Place the mixture in a mold and place in the freezer. Serve frozen.

Serves 4
Preparation Time:
  20 Minutes
(note freezing time)

 10 egg yolks
  2 eggs
1½ cups powdered sugar
 ½ cup peppermint
    schnapps
  3 Tbsps. fresh mint,
    chopped
 ½ cup chocolate shavings
  1 qt. whipped cream

BROUSSARD'S

Broussard's
CONTINENTAL AND CREOLE CUISINE
819 Conti Street
New Orleans, Louisiana
(504) 581-3866
Dinner 5:30PM–10PM
AVERAGE DINNER FOR TWO: $70

Broussard's is one of the Grand Dames of restaurants in New Orleans—a tradition for more than 75 years. Proprietors Gunter and Evelyn Preuss have dedicated their restaurant to perfecting the art of Creole cooking, the most unique indigenous American cuisine.

That means starters such as Crab Meat Ravigote, Shrimp with Two Remoulades and oysters any way you like them, followed by mouthwatering entrees, including Pompano Napoleon, Filet Mignon Josephine and a house specialty, Veal Broussard, and luscious desserts ranging from Bread Pudding with Whiskey Sauce to Bananas Foster.

At Broussard's you will find ambiance and exemplary service equally important in the art of fine dining. Enjoy a New Orleans specialty cocktail—a Sazerac or perhaps a Vin Blanc Cassis—in the peaceful setting of the courtyard with the fragrance of wisteria and night-blooming jasmine.

BROUSSARD'S MENU FOR SIX

Shrimp and Crab Meat Cheesecake

Crab Meat Broussard's

Pecan Stuffed Salmon

Shrimp and Crab Meat Cheesecake

I n a large bowl, combine the mayonnaise, sour cream, lemon juice, mustard, 3 Tbsps. dill, tarragon, garlic, green onion and paprika. Mix well until everything is incorporated. Fold in the chopped shrimp. Set aside.

Mix the cider vinegar and gelatin in a small skillet and place over medium heat, stirring constantly until gelatin dissolves. Pour the gelatin slowly into the shrimp mixture and mix well. Quickly but gently fold crab meat into mixture and pour into 8-inch springform pan. Cover and refrigerate overnight.

Drain the pimientos and place in a blender with heavy cream, cream cheese and salt. Purée. Pour into a glass bowl and mix in 2 Tbsps. dill. Cover and refrigerate overnight.

To make the pecan mixture, melt the butter in a skillet. Add the pecans, salt, cayenne and Worcestershire. Sauté 2 to 3 minutes but do not burn the mixture. Cool and rough chop. Do not refrigerate.

Remove sides of the springform pan and spread the pimiento sauce over the top of the cheesecake. Take the chopped pecans and press into the sides of the cheesecake. Chill until ready to serve.

Cooking Secret: This dish is not only a great appetizer, but served with a mixed green salad, it makes a perfect lunch entrée.

Serves 6
Preparation Time:
  45 Minutes
(note refrigeration time)

  2 cups mayonnaise
  2 cups sour cream
  4 Tbsps. fresh lemon
    juice
  8 Tbsps. Dijon mustard
  3 Tbsps. fresh dill,
    chopped
  2 tsps. tarragon leaves
  2 tsps. roasted garlic,
    minced
  1 cup green onion, sliced
  2 tsps. paprika
  ¾ lb. cooked shrimp,
    peeled, chopped
  10 Tbsps. cider vinegar
  7½ Tbsps. unflavored
    gelatin
  ¼ lb. crab meat, jumbo
    lump
  1 14 oz. can whole red
    pimientos, about
    2 cups
  ½ cup heavy cream
  8 oz. cream cheese
  1½ tsps. salt
  2 Tbsps. dill
  2 Tbsps. butter
  1 cup pecan pieces
    Salt to taste
    Pinch of cayenne
    pepper
  1 tsp. Worcestershire
    sauce

☆

Crab Meat Broussard's

Serves 6
Preparation Time:
  45 Minutes
Preheat oven to 400°

  1 Tbsp. butter
  6 Jumbo shrimp, peeled,
     butterflied
  5 Tbsps. olive oil
  1 small onion, diced
  2 artichoke hearts,
     chopped
  1 garlic clove, minced
  ¼ cup flour
  ¼ cup white wine
  2 cups chicken stock
  1 cup heavy cream
  3 oz. Brie cheese
  ½ cup bread crumbs
  1 Tbsp. whole thyme
     leaves
  ¾ lb. crab meat, jumbo
     lump

I n a large skillet, melt the butter and sauté the shrimp. Set aside to cool.

In a heavy saucepan, heat 2 Tbsps. olive oil and sauté the onion, artichoke and garlic over medium heat until the onion becomes limp. Sprinkle in the flour and mix well. Deglaze with white wine, then add the stock. Reduce the heat and simmer for 3 minutes. Add the heavy cream and simmer another 5 minutes. Remove from heat and let stand 2 to 3 minutes.

Take the Brie and scrape off the white "skin" and cut into small pieces. Add the Brie to the cream sauce and stir until all cheese is melted and mixed well. Let cool.

Mix the bread crumbs, thyme and 3 Tbsps. olive oil. Set aside.

After cheese mixture has cooled, gently fold in the crab meat. Place one shrimp in the center of a 2½ oz. ovenproof dish, so that it stands. If you have a problem, make the butterfly cut deeper. Spoon the crab meat mixture around the shrimp and sprinkle with bread crumb mixture. Repeat with remaining shrimps in remaining dishes.

Place dishes on a cooking pan and place in a 400° oven for 15 to 20 minutes or until hot and bubbly.

☆

Pecan Stuffed Salmon

I n a mixing bowl, combine the bread crumbs, pecan pieces, parsley, onion, zest and juice, butter and seasonings. Set aside.

Take the filets and cut a pocket down the middle and into the sides. Stuff the filets with the pecan mixture.

Bake in a 400° oven for about 10 minutes.

Serves 6
Preparation Time:
  20 Minutes
Preheat oven to 400°

- 4 cups bread crumbs, finely chopped
- 4 cups pecan pieces
- 2 cups parsley, chopped
- 2 cups green onion, thinly sliced
- ½ cup lemon zest
- 1 cup lemon juice
- 4 cups soft butter
  Cayenne pepper to taste
  Salt and pepper to taste
- 6 salmon fillets, 6 oz. each

GALATOIRE'S

Galatoire's
FRENCH-CREOLE CUISINE
209 Bourbon Street
New Orleans, Louisiana
(504) 525-2021
Lunch and Dinner Daily 11:30AM–9PM
AVERAGE DINNER FOR TWO: $70

T rendy places come and go, but certain traditions endure in New Orleans. For Friday lunch, Galatoire's is the place. It's the place to see and be seen and, of course, to eat. There is a sense of excitement and joie de vivre at Galatoire's. Diners often say it feels like Mardi Gras. It's a party in the splendor of one of the city's landmarks.

Family-owned and operated since 1905, Galatoire's prides itself on the fact that its traditions remain constant throughout the eras. With mirrored walls, white tile floors, chandeliers and brass fixtures, it is one of the prettiest restaurants in New Orleans. The service is impeccable—waiters serve you in tuxedos!

Galatoire's specialties include Shrimp Rémoulade, Chicken Clemenceau, Sirloin Marchand de Vin, Broccoli Hollandaise and Crêpes Maison. The menu also includes Crab Meat Cocktails, Stuffed Avocado with Crabmeat Salad, Stuffed Tomato with Shrimp Salad, a Portobello Mushroom Platter, Rockefeller Spinach, Cherries Jubilee, Crêpes Suzette and a wonderful Chocolate Nut Sundae.

GALATOIRE'S MENU FOR FOUR

Crab Meat Maison

Oysters en Brochette

Trout Meunière Amandine

Crab Meat Maison

Mix mayonnaise, French dressing, onions, capers, and parsley together. Once thoroughly mixed, fold in the crab meat. Serve over a bed of lettuce with two slices of tomato on the sides. Squeeze lemon juice over salad just before serving.

Serves 6
Preparation Time:
  30 Minutes

½ cup homemade
   mayonnaise
3 Tbsps. French dressing
   (olive oil, vinegar,
   Creole mustard, salt
   and pepper to taste)
3 green onions, finely
   chopped
1 tsp. capers
½ tsp. parsley, chopped
1 lb. crab meat
12 lettuce slices
12 tomato slices
   Juice from 1 lemon

Oysters en Brochette

Serves 4
Preparation Time:
  15 Minutes

   12 bacon strips, cut in
       half
    2 dozen raw oysters
    4 skewers, 8-inches each
    1 egg
   ¾ cup milk
       Salt and pepper to
       taste
    2 cups flour
       Oil for deep frying
    4 bread slices, toasted
    2 lemons, cut in wedges,
       garnish

Fry bacon until not quite crisp. Alternate 6 oysters and 6 half strips of bacon (folded) on each skewer. Beat together egg and milk and seasoning well with salt and pepper. Dip each skewer in egg and milk mixture, roll in flour and deep fry until golden. Serve on toast with lemon wedges.

☆

Trout Meunière Amandine

Salt and pepper trout fillets and dip in milk, then roll in flour. Fry in hot oil in a shallow pan until golden on both sides.

In a separate pan, melt and continuously whip butter until brown and frothy. Add almonds and lemon juice. Pour over trout. Garnish with parsley.

Serves 4
Preparation Time:
  30 Minutes

  4 **speckled trout fillets,**
    6 to 8 oz. each
    Salt and pepper to
    taste
  1 **cup milk**
  1 **cup flour**
    Oil for frying
  ½ **lb. butter**
  4 **oz. almonds, sliced,**
    toasted
    Juice of 1 lemon
  ½ **Tbsp. parsley, chopped,**
    garnish

JOE'S "DREYFUS STORE" RESTAURANT

Joe's "Dreyfus Store" Restaurant
LOUISIANA CUISINE
Highway 77 South
Livonia, Louisiana
(504) 637-2625
Lunch Tuesday–Sunday 11AM–2PM
Dinner Tuesday–Saturday 5PM–9PM
AVERAGE DINNER FOR TWO: $50

I t's not the kind of place you just run across. Someone has to tell you about this restaurant. No fuss, just great flavor, offering traditional recipes for Shrimp Remoulade, Fried Oysters, Joe's Fried Fresh Fat Soft-Shell Crabs or the Catfish Breaux Bridge, a fried whole catfish on rice, swimming in crawfish étouffée.

Step through the door onto old wood floors, with farm implements and framed hodgepodge on the walls, to a big room of tables with plates mounded high with traditional Louisiana cuisine. This site has been the Dreyfus General Store since the 1890s. The restaurant run by Louisiana natives Joe and Diane Major draws rave reviews as well as crowds from miles around.

JOE'S "DREYFUS STORE" RESTAURANT MENU FOR SIX

Marinated Crab Fingers

Corn and Shrimp Soup

Bread Pudding with Rum Sauce

Marinated Crab Fingers

n a mixing bowl combine the crab meat with the oils, lemon juice, vinegar, onion, celery, carrot and seasonings. Mix well and chill for 24 hours before serving.

Serves 6
Preparation Time:
  5 Minutes
(note marinating time)

  5 lbs. crab fingers (crab meat)
  1 cup vegetable oil
  4 Tbsps. olive oil
  ¼ cup lemon juice
  4 Tbsps. vinegar
  1 onion, thinly sliced
  1 stalk celery, thinly sliced
  1 carrot, thinly sliced
    Dash of Worcestershire sauce
    Salt and pepper to taste
    Red pepper to taste

☆

Corn and Shrimp Soup

Serves 6
Preparation Time:
  45 Minutes

  4 oz. salt pork belly,
    diced, optional
  1 large onion, diced
  1 large bell pepper, diced
  ½ stalk celery, diced
  1 stick butter
  2 Tbsps. flour
  2 qts. shrimp stock
  1 lb. fresh ripe tomatoes,
    peeled, seeded,
    chopped
    Salt and pepper to
    taste
  2 lbs. small shrimp,
    heads on, or 1 lb. small
    shrimp, peeled

Sauté the diced pork until lightly browned. Add the onion, bell pepper, celery and butter. Cook until the onion is translucent. Add the flour. Cook for 5 minutes, stirring.

Add the shrimp stock, corn, tomatoes and seasoning. Simmer for 25 minutes. Add the shrimp and simmer for 10 more minutes. Season to taste before serving.

☆

Bread Pudding with Rum Sauce

In a large bowl, combine the sugar, cinnamon, nutmeg, vanilla, eggs and egg yolks with a hand whip. Add the milk, raisins and coconut and stir until thoroughly combined.

Add the bread slices, gently pushing them down into the milk mixture. Do not squeeze. Let the slices soak for 30 minutes, turning occasionally.

In a small bowl, cream the butter and powdered sugar. Generously coat the sides and bottom of a 9 × 13 × 2-inch cake pan (preferably glass) with half the butter-sugar mixture. Reserve the other half.

Pour the pudding into the prepared pan. Pat down. Gently push raisins into the mixture so they will not burn in the oven.

Melt the remaining butter-sugar mixture. Pour on top of the pudding.

Place the pan on a cookie sheet and bake at 325° for 45 to 50 minutes in the top third of the oven. Allow pudding to cool before serving.

For the sauce: In a small saucepan, combine the butter, powdered sugar and cream. Bring to a boil over medium heat, stirring constantly. Remove from heat and add the rum. Cool and pour on top of pudding before serving.

Serves 6
Preparation Time:
  1¼ Hours
Preheat oven to 325°

  2 cups sugar
  ½ tsp. ground cinnamon
     Pinch of nutmeg
  1 tsp. vanilla
  4 eggs plus 2 egg yolks
  1 qt. whole milk
  ½ cup raisins
  1 cup sweet coconut,
     shredded
  1 loaf day-old French
     bread, cut into ½-inch
     slices
  4 Tbsps. soft unsalted
     butter
  4 Tbsps. powdered sugar

Rum Sauce:
  4 Tbsps. unsalted butter
  ½ cup powdered sugar
  ½ cup whipping cream
  1 Tbsp. Myer's dark rum

LAFITTE'S LANDING

Lafitte's Landing
FRENCH AND CAJUN CUISINE
10275 Highway 70 Access
St. James, Louisiana
(504) 473-1232
Lunch 11AM–3PM
Dinner 6PM–10PM
Sunday Brunch 11AM–3PM
AVERAGE DINNER FOR TWO: $55

Almost 200 years ago a legend was born. His name was Jean Lafitte. The name of this legend is about all that historians can agree on. There is disagreement about his birthplace, marriage (or marriages) and even the time and place of his death. But there is no disagreement that Jean Lafitte was the most colorful character in the entire history of Louisiana. He was denounced as a pirate, a scoundrel and a smuggler. He was admired as a corsair, a privateer and a gentleman rover. Poets signed for the man who committed "a thousand villainies and a single heroism."

Chef John Folse acquired the Old Viala Plantation home in 1978, when it was moved to its present site at the western approach to the Sunshine Bridge, and established his Lafitte's Landing Restaurant with his indigenous Louisiana cuisine. Menu highlights include a thick wedge of fresh Tuna that is Charbroiled and topped with Grilled Shrimp and Roasted Tomato Salsa on Tequila Lime Butter. The Fresh Salmon Fillets are rubbed with Citrus and Horseradish, then topped with Pan-Fried Scallops on Julienned Vegetables. A Roasted Herb-Encrusted Rack of Lamb is served with Caramelized Sweet Potatoes and Mayhaw Pepper Jelly Glacé and the 10-oz. Veal Chop is Pan-Roasted and served with a Wild Mushroom Flan and Roasted Shallot Glace. Absolutely delicious.

LAFITTE'S LANDING'S MENU FOR SIX

Louisiana Seafood Gumbo

Cajun Stuffed Rack of Lamb

Orange Cane Syrup Pecan Pie

Louisiana Seafood Gumbo

I n a 7-qt. cast-iron Dutch oven, heat the oil over medium-high heat. Sprinkle in the flour and using a wire whisk, stir constantly until a brown roux is achieved. Do not allow the roux to scorch. Should black specks appear in the roux, discard and begin again.

Once the roux is golden brown, add the onions, celery, bell pepper, garlic and sausage. Sauté for approximately 3 to 5 minutes. Stir the claw crab meat into the roux. This will begin to add the seafood flavor to the mixture. Slowly add hot shellfish stock, one ladle at a time, stirring constantly until all is incorporated.

Bring to a low boil, reduce to simmer and cook approximately 30 minutes. Add additional stock if necessary to retain volume.

Add green onions and parsley. Season to taste using salt, pepper and Louisiana Gold. Fold shrimp, lump crab meat, oysters and reserved oyster liquid into soup.

Return to a low boil and cook approximately 5 minutes. Adjust seasoning and serve over cooked rice.

Serves 6
Preparation Time:
 1 Hour

- 1 **cup vegetable oil**
- 1 **cup flour**
- 2 **cups onions, chopped**
- 1 **cup celery, chopped**
- 1 **cup bell pepper, chopped**
- ¼ **cup garlic, diced**
- ½ **lb. Andouille sausage, sliced**
- 1 **lb. claw crab meat**
- 3 **qts. shellfish stock**
- 2 **cups green onions, sliced**
- ½ **cup parsley, chopped**
  Salt and cayenne pepper to taste
  Louisiana Gold Pepper Sauce to taste, optional
- 1 **lb. shrimp, peeled, deveined**
- 1 **lb. jumbo lump crab meat**
- 24 **oysters, shucked (reserve liquid)**
- 6 **cups rice, cooked**

★

Cajun Stuffed Rack of Lamb

Serves 6
Preparation Time:
 1 Hour

 6 lamb racks
   Salt and pepper to
   taste
 1 cup shrimp, cooked,
   chopped
 1 cup claw crab meat
 ¼ cup onions, finely
   diced
 ¼ cup green onions,
   finely diced
 1 Tbsp. garlic, diced
 1 Tbsp. red bell pepper,
   diced
 ½ cup béchamel sauce
 ½ cup seasoned Italian
   bread crumbs
   Salt and cayenne
   pepper to taste

Seasonings:
 ¼ cup butter, melted
 2 Tbsps. dried thyme
 2 Tbsps. dried basil
 1 Tbsp. dried tarragon
 1 Tbsp. crushed
   rosemary
 2 Tbsps. garlic, diced
   Salt and cracked black
   pepper to taste
 1 cup red wine
 3 cups demi-glace

Using a 6-inch paring knife, cut a ¾-inch slit in the center of the lamb loin. Be sure not to cut completely through the meat. The pocket should be large enough to hold a generous portion of the stuffing. Lightly season the inside of the pocket with salt and pepper. Set aside.

In a large mixing bowl, combine the shrimp, crab, onions, garlic, bell pepper, béchamel sauce and bread crumbs, blending well to ensure that all seasonings are evenly mixed. Season to taste using salt and pepper. The stuffing should be moist but stiff enough to stand on its own. Add more bread crumbs or béchamel if necessary. Stuff each loin with an equal amount of the seafood stuffing. Set aside.

Seasonings:

On a large baking pan with a 1-inch lip, place stuffed lamb racks. Moisten with melted butter and season generously with thyme, basil, tarragon, rosemary and garlic. Season to taste using salt and cracked black pepper.

Place the racks on the baking pan, bone side up and bake approximately 25 minutes for medium-rare. Remove from oven and deglaze the baking pan with red wine, making sure to scrape bottom well.

Pour these ingredients into a 10-inch sauté pan and add demi-glace. Bring to a boil and reduce until slightly thickened. Using a sharp knife, slice lamb racks into four chops each and top with a generous portion of demi-glace.

Orange Cane Syrup Pecan Pie

In a large mixing bowl, combine eggs and sugar. Using a wire whisk, whip until well-blended. Do not over-beat. Add the Karo and cane syrups, blending into the egg mixture. Add the orange juice, orange peel and flour. Blend until all is well incorporated. Add the chopped pecans and fold once or twice into the mixture. Pour mixture into pie shells.

Place the pecan halves in a circular pattern on the outer edges of the pie. Place pies on a cookie sheet covered with parchment paper.

Bake approximately 1 hour and check for doneness. It is best to cool the pies overnight before serving.

Yield:
  2 pies
Preparation Time:
  1¼ Hours
Preheat oven to 350°

  10 **eggs**
   1 **cup sugar**
   2 **cups light Karo syrup**
   1 **Tbsp. cane syrup**
  ½ **cup freshly squeezed orange juice**
   1 **Tbsp. orange peel, grated**
   2 **Tbsps. flour**
  1½ **cups pecans, chopped**
   2 **unbaked 10-inch pie shells**
  16 **pecan halves**

PALACE CAFÉ

Palace Café
CONTEMPORARY CREOLE SEAFOOD
605 Canal Street
New Orleans, Louisiana
(504) 523-1661
AVERAGE DINNER FOR TWO: $75

The Palace Café is the New Orleans version of one of the grand cafés of Paris. The food is real basic food that stays within the boundaries of New Orleans tradition. Chef Robert Bruce focuses his menu to highlight local ingredients, which means you won't find any foie gras and truffles. The food is clean, straightforward, less fussy and definitely a lot cheaper.

Some of the must-tries on the menu are a Pan-Roasted Oyster appetizer, poached in a light Rosemary-Infused Cream, then topped with Romano Cheese and Bread Crumbs. Bruce's Gumbo is brimming with flavors enhanced with Gulf Seafood, Okra, Peppers and Garlic. The Soft-Shell Crabs are flash-fried until crisp, then served with a fragrant Ragout made from fresh Corn and Mirlitons and finished off with a Spicy Hot Tasso Ham and drizzled with a Hollandaise spiked with Red Onions.

One section of the menu is devoted to tempting entrée salads offering a choice of Jumbo Shrimp in Rémoulade Dressing with Roasted Tomatoes on a bed of Baby Greens, or a Roasted Chicken tossed with a Citrus Essence, Creole Mustard, Spinach, Pepper and Roasted Pecans or Bruce's signature Crabmeat Cheesecake in a pool of Creole Sauce Meunière atop baby lettuce with a light drizzle of Balsamic-Lime Vinaigrette.

Save room for desserts, with tempting selections such as the Louisiana Root Beer Float with housemade sugar-cane ice cream and Bananas Foster Shortcake, Bourbon Pecan Pie and the famous White Chocolate Bread Pudding, created with white chocolate baked inside the bread pudding and smothered with a warm white chocolate sauce.

PALACE CAFÉ'S MENU FOR FOUR

Oyster Six Shot

Bouillabaisse with Herb Croutons and Rouille Sauce

Mango, Strawberry and Opal Basil Sorbet

Oyster Six Shot

For the Peppercorn Mignonette: Combine all the ingredients except the oil in a blender. With the blender still running, slowly add the oil to emulsify. Set aside.

For the Cajun-Mary Sauce: In a mixing bowl combine all the ingredients. Season to taste with salt, pepper and Creole seasoning.

To assemble, place 1 oyster in each of the 24 shot glasses. Top 12 of the oysters with 1 Tbsp. of the Peppercorn Mignotte. Top the other 12 with 1 Tbsp. of the Cajun-Mary Sauce.

Place 6 shot glasses on each of 4 large plates: 3 with Peppercorn Mignonette and 3 with Cajun-Mary Sauce. Garnish with a lemon crown in the center of the plate and a sprinkling of parsley.

Serves 4
Preparation Time:
  45 Minutes

Peppercorn Mignonette:
Yield: 1½ cups
  2 shallots, peeled,
    minced
  ½ cup red wine vinegar
  5 Tbsps. Creole mustard
  1 Tbsp. cracked black
    pepper
  1 tsp. salt
1½ cups salad oil

Cajun-Mary Sauce:
Yield: 1½ cups
  1 cup tomato juice
  ½ cup tomato paste
  1 tsp. Tabasco sauce
  3 Tbsps. Worcestershire
    sauce
  ¼ cup lemon juice
  ½ tsp. ground celery
    seeds
    Salt and ground black
    pepper to taste
    Creole seasoning to
    taste

24 raw oysters
  4 lemon crowns, garnish
  1 Tbsp. parsley, chopped,
    garnish
24 chilled shot glasses

Bouillabaisse with Herb Croutons and Rouille Sauce

Serves 4
Preparation Time:
  45 Minutes
(note refrigeration time)

  1 Tbsp. olive oil
  2 cups fennel, julienned
  2 cups leeks, sliced
  3 Tbsps. garlic, chopped
  1 sprig fresh thyme
  1 tsp. saffron
  2 oz. Herbsaint*
  2 tomatoes, chopped
  ½ cup tomato paste
  6 cups clam juice
    Salt to taste
  ¼ tsp. cayenne pepper
  16 clams
  16 mussels
  32 shrimp, 40/50 size
  ¼ lb. calamari
  24 oysters
    Herb Croutons (recipe
    follows)
    Rouille Sauce (recipe
    follows)

In a large sauce pot, heat the olive oil. Sear the fennel and leeks, stirring constantly. Reduce heat and cover the pot, letting the fennel and leeks sweat until wilted. Add the garlic, thyme and saffron. Cook for 5 minutes.

Deglaze the vegetables with Herbsaint. Add the tomatoes and tomato paste and cook for 5 minutes on low heat.

Add the clam juice and let simmer for an additional 10 minutes. Season with salt and cayenne pepper; taste and re-season if needed. Chill thoroughly.

Before serving, bring the sauce to a boil in a large sauce pot. Add the clams and let simmer for 1 minute. Add the mussels and let simmer for another minute. Next, add the shrimp and continue to simmer for another 30 seconds. Last, add the calamari and oysters and allow to simmer for 1 minute. Taste and re-season with salt if necessary.

Serve in large soup bowls. Garnish with Herb Croutons and Rouille Sauce (recipes follow).

Cooking Secret: Make the soup one day ahead to allow flavors to develop.

* Herbsaint is an anise-flavored liqueur developed and made primarily in New Orleans.

☆

Herb Croutons

Slice the French bread into 1-inch thick rounds. Toss the rounds with olive oil, basil and oregano in a large mixing bowl to coat the bread.

Lay croutons out in a single layer on an ungreased sheet pan. Toast in a 350° oven until just crisp. Let cool.

When the croutons have cooled to room temperature, spread each with 2 tsps. of the Rouille Sauce (recipe follows) and serve with bouillabaisse.

Preparation Time:
 10 Minutes
Preheat oven to 350°

 1 **loaf French bread**
 ¼ **cup olive oil**
 ½ **Tbsp. dried oregano**
 ½ **Tbsp. dried basil**

Rouille Sauce

Yield:
  1 cup

  1 red pepper, blanched, seeded, skinned, or 1 can pimientos
  1 tsp. hot sauce
  ¼ cup white bread crumbs, soaked in water and squeezed dry
  2 garlic cloves, mashed
  ¼ cup olive oil

 n a small mixing bowl, blend together the pepper, hot sauce, bread crumbs and garlic to a paste. Very slowly, beat in the olive oil for a mayonnaise-like consistency.

Mango, Strawberry and Opal Basil Sorbet

Clean and hull the strawberries. Sprinkle with sugar and toss to coat berries.

Combine the mango purée, lime juice and syrup in a large bowl.

Purée the basil with a small amount of syrup mixture in a blender and strain to remove the basil leaves, then return purée to the rest of the syrup mixture.

Purée the strawberries in a blender and strain, removing all fibers. Add the berries to the syrup mixture and combine.

Process according to ice cream machine instructions. Freeze for 24 hours.

Yield:
  2 quarts
Preparation Time:
  30 Minutes
(note freezing time)

  8 **cups strawberries**
  ½ **cup sugar**
  2 **cups mango purée**
  1 **cup fresh lime juice**
  3 **cups simple syrup**
    (equal parts sugar and
    water by volume)
  ¼ **Tbsp. opal basil**

PREJEAN'S

Prejean's
NOUVEAU CAJUN CUISINE
3480 Highway 167 North
Carencro, Louisiana
(318) 896-3247
AVERAGE DINNER FOR TWO: $35

Upon entering Prejean's Restaurant you notice a glass display case filled with more than 120 state and national culinary medals, many of them gold medals. Executive Chef James Graham is widely recognized as one of the best Cajun chefs in the country—the irony being that he is originally from Montana and taught himself how to prepare Cajun dishes while working in Florida.

Graham describes his approach to cooking as "Infusion Cuisine," a blend of the best elements of Louisiana Creole, French and Cajun cooking. It taps into a growing trend in American cooking, he says. "As Americans have developed a taste for the deep and complex flavors of wine, they've looked to marry those wines with foods that have equally deep and intense flavors, like the rich and spicy sauces of South Louisiana."

PREJEAN'S MENU FOR SIX

Trio of Wild Mushrooms and Smoked Duckling Soup

Crawfish Étouffée

Crescent City Quail

Trio of Wild Mushrooms and Smoked Duckling Soup

Brown the duck bones in a 350° oven. Add the butter, leeks, carrots, parsnips, onion and garlic cloves. Stir well and continue to cook for 25 minutes, stirring often. Add the water and chicken stock and transfer the pan to the stove's top burner. Bring to a boil and cook at a low boil for 15 minutes. Strain the stock, discarding the leeks, onion and bones.

Reserve the carrots and parsnips. Dice them fine and set aside.

Bring the stock to a boil. Add a pinch of black and white pepper, cayenne pepper, thyme and bay leaf.

In a pan, melt the butter and sauté the mushrooms, cooking for 3 minutes. Add the flour and cook for 2 minutes.

Add the mushrooms to the boiling stock and stir until the roux dissolves from the mushrooms. Add the cooked duck, the reserved parsnips and carrots and the cream.

Serves 6
Preparation Time:
1 Hour
Preheat oven to 350°

3 hickory smoked cooked ducklings, deboned, reserving bones for stock
½ lb. butter
2 leeks
2 carrots
2 parsnips
1 onion
3 garlic cloves
3 qts. water
1 qt. rich chicken stock
Black and white pepper to taste
¼ tsp. cayenne pepper
¼ tsp. fresh thyme
1 bay leaf
4 Tbsps. butter
¾ cup whole morels
¾ cup whole chanterelles
½ cup shiitakes, sliced
3 Tbsps. flour
¼ cup heavy cream

Crawfish Étouffée

Serves 6
Preparation Time:
  30 Minutes

  3 sticks butter
  ⅓ cup flour
  2 small onions, finely
    diced
  ⅓ cup celery, finely diced
  ⅔ cup bell pepper, finely
    diced
  ¼ cup green onion
    bottoms
  2 Tbsps. paprika
  1 tsp. cayenne pepper
  1 tsp. black pepper
  ¾ tsp. garlic
  3 Tbsps. chicken
    bouillon
  2 lbs. crawfish tails
  2 Tbsps. parsley,
    chopped
  ½ cup green onion tops

ombine 1 stick butter and flour in a small saucepan. Stir while cooking for 3 minutes over medium-high heat to make a roux.

In a 4-quart saucepan, melt 1 stick butter and all onions, celery, bell pepper, green onion bottoms, spices, garlic and chicken bouillon. Cook for 2 more minutes while stirring. Add 1 qt. water and bring to a boil, boiling for 5 minutes.

Add the roux, stirring well with a wire whip. Reduce heat to medium and boil another 3 minutes.

Add the crawfish tails, onion tops and parsley. Add the last stick of butter and turn heat to low until ready to serve.

Note: This recipe won the 1994 World Étouffée Championship.

Crescent City Quail

Combine ingredients in a large mixing bowl and marinate quail for 1 hour.

For the mousse: In the food processor, purée the Cornish hen breasts. Place in a cold bowl with ice underneath it.

Purée the onions and add to the bowl. Add to the boil the mushrooms, chopped rosemary, chicken base, heavy whipping cream, garlic powder and cayenne pepper. With an electric mixer or by hand, whip all ingredients until cream sets, or about 4 to 5 minutes. Remove bowl to table.

With a rubber spatula, fold in the egg whites. Place the mousse in a pastry bag for stuffing the quail.

Remove the quail from the marinade and fill each quail's breast cavity with 4 Tbsps. of the wild mushroom and Cornish hen mousse.

Grill the stuffed quail, marking both sides with grill marks. Transfer to a baking sheet and finish in the oven at 350° for 8 to 10 minutes.

Slice each quail breast into 2 medallions, placing the body in the center of the plate, fanning medallions out.

Serves 6
Preparation Time:
   1 Hour
(note marinating time)
Preheat oven to 350°

Marinade:
   1 tsp. all-purpose Cajun seasoning
   1 Tbsp. Worcestershire sauce
   ¼ cup Bordeaux wine
   1 tsp. garlic, minced
   12 semi-boneless quail

Mousse:
   16 oz. Cornish hen breasts
   ¼ cup onion
   ½ cup morels, sliced
   2 tsps. fresh rosemary needles, chopped
   2 tsps. chicken base
   ½ cup heavy whipping cream
   ¼ tsp. garlic powder
   ¼ tsp. cayenne pepper
   2 egg whites, beaten to soft peaks and set aside in the refrigerator

PRUDHOMME'S CAJUN CAFÉ

Prudhomme's Cajun Café
CAJUN CUISINE
4676 N. E. Evangeline Throughway
Carencro, Louisiana
(318) 869-7964
Lunch and Dinner Monday–Saturday 11AM–10PM
AVERAGE DINNER FOR TWO: $45

Enola Prudhomme and her family serve up authentic Cajun cuisine that's been associated with Louisiana and the Prudhomme name throughout the world for years. If you want the genuine food, this is the place–housed in a building constructed in the late 1800s.

Chef Prudhomme understands Cajun cuisine from the ground up, thanks to her family heritage. Along with her 11 sisters and brothers (including celebrity Chef Paul), she published "Prudhomme's Family Cookbook" and has won countless awards and medals for her menus.

Specialties include wonderful sautéed, fried and blackened Cajun dishes, pastas, steaks, low-fat entrees, homemade jalapeño bread, muffins, salads and desserts. Some of the highlights are her award-winning Catfish Enola, Pan-Fried Stuffed Catfish with Shrimp and Tasso Cream Sauce, Stuffed Red Snapper, Eggplant Rounds with Tasso Gravy and Pecan Cake.

PRUDHOMME'S CAJUN CAFÉ'S MENU FOR FOUR

Broccoli Soup

Shrimp Pasta

Dutch Apple Cake

Broccoli Soup

In a large pot, bring water to a boil over high heat. Add the broccoli and continue to boil for about 20 minutes. Remove from heat and reserve 1 cup of the water; discard remaining water.

Place drained broccoli in a food processor and pulse until chopped. Do not over-process.

In a large pot over high heat, bring the whipping cream, canned milk and reserved cup of water to a boil. Reduce the heat to medium. Add the broccoli, salt and pepper; cook and stir for 15 minutes.

Melt butter in a medium skillet over medium heat. Add the flour. Cook and stir constantly until the flour turns the color of caramel. Remove from heat and slowly add to the broccoli mixture until soup is the desired thickness.

Serves 4
Preparation Time:
   45 Minutes

   8 cups water
   8 cups fresh broccoli
      florets
1½ qts. heavy whipping
      cream
   3 cups canned
      evaporated milk
2½ tsps. salt
   ⅛ tsp. ground red pepper
   ¼ cup unsalted butter
   ½ cup all-purpose flour

★

Shrimp Pasta

Serves 4
Preparation Time:
 30 Minutes

 1 lb. rotini pasta
 ¼ cup butter or
   margarine
 1 lb. medium shrimp,
   peeled, deveined
 2 tsps. seafood seasoning
 ⅓ cup shrimp stock or
   water
 ½ cup chopped green
   onion tops
 ¾ cup fresh mushrooms,
   sliced thin
 1 pint heavy whipping
   cream

C ook the pasta according to package directions; set aside.

Over high heat, melt the butter in a 5-quart pot. Add the shrimp and 1 tsp. of the seasoning; cook and stir 2 minutes. Stir in the stock, or water and cook 7 minutes. Add the onion tops, mushrooms, remaining seasoning and whipping cream. Cook over medium heat for 6 to 8 minutes. Add the pasta to the shrimp and reduce heat to low. Cook for 3 more minutes.

☆

Dutch Apple Cake

Arrange the apple slices in a greased 9-inch square baking pan. Sprinkle the apples with brown sugar and pour 4 Tbsps. melted butter over the apple mixture.

In a medium bowl combine the flour, baking powder, salt and sugar. Stir well to mix.

In a separate bowl, blend together the egg, milk, vanilla, the remaining melted butter and the apple spice. Slowly add to the flour mixture. With a hand mixer on high speed, beat for 30 seconds or until the mixture is nice and fluffy. Pour the batter over the sliced apples and bake at 375° for 40 to 50 minutes. After removing from the oven, immediately loosen the cake from the sides of the pan. Turn upside down on a cake plate or board before serving.

Serves 8
Preparation Time:
  1 Hour
Preheat oven to 375°

  2 **cups sliced cooking**
      apples
  ½ **cup dark brown sugar**
  ½ **cup melted butter**
  1¼ **cups all-purpose flour**
  1¼ **tsps. baking powder**
  ¼ **tsp. salt**
  ¾ **cup granulated sugar**
  1 **egg, beaten**
  ½ **cup milk**
  ½ **tsp. vanilla extract**
  1 **tsp. apple spice**

☆

FLEUR DI LIS BED AND BREAKFAST

Fleur di Lis Bed and Breakfast
336 Second Street
Natchitoches, Louisiana 71457
(800) 489-6621
(318) 352-6621
ROOM RATES: $60–$100

F leur di Lis, named after the royal symbol of France, is a charming Queen Ann Victorian house built in 1903. The bed and breakfast home offers spacious surroundings tastefully decorated with antiques and Victorian accents. In addition to beautiful woodwork such as massive cypress doors and ornamental molding, the inn has a grand, old-fashioned, wraparound porch, complete with rockers and a swing.

Five guest rooms, each with a private bath and a king- or queen-sized bed, are available. A full breakfast is served at their 12-foot-long Louisiana cypress table. Some of the favorite recipes of guests are goodies such as French Toast, Sausage Breakfast Casserole and Louisiana Breakfast Casserole.

Located in the Historic District, the inn is within walking distance of shops, restaurants, Northwestern State University of Louisiana and plantations along River Road.

French Toast

Spray or oil a 13 × 9-inch baking dish with Pam or any vegetable spray.

Cut bread into 1-inch slices and arrange in one layer in the dish.

In a mixing bowl, combine the milk, eggs, sugar, salt, vanilla, melted butter and nutmeg. Pour over the bread. Cover and refrigerate overnight.

Next morning, uncover and bake at 350° for 45 minutes or until puffy and browned.

Let stand for 5 minutes. Serve with warmed, flavored syrups or honey butter.

Serves 6 to 8
Preparation Time:
  45 Minutes
(note refrigeration time)
Preheat oven to 350°

  1 loaf French bread
  3 cups milk
  8 eggs
  4 tsps. sugar
  ¾ tsp. salt
1½ Tbsps. vanilla
  3 Tbsps. butter, melted
  ¼ tsp. nutmeg

☆

HOTEL MAISON DE VILLE

Hotel Maison de Ville
727 Rue Toulouse
New Orleans, Louisiana 70130
(800) 634-1600
(504) 561-5858
ROOM RATES: $165–$825

I n the heart of the French Quarter, Maison de Ville is one of the most romantic desti-
nations in the country. High ceilings, antiques, four-poster beds and period paintings
are just some of the touches that give the main house a luxurious feeling. Accommodations
reflect a different phase of the genteel Southern lifestyle: some are refined, some are rustic. The
antiques are individualized and fit each setting.

Built circa 1788 by American naturalist John James Audubon for his family, the Audubon
Cottages are where he created many of his wildlife masterpieces. All the historic cottages, situated around a swimming pool, have private courtyards, rare antiques and Audubon prints.

The Bistro at Maison de Ville is small, but the experience is luscious, flavorful and diverse.
The white-clothed tables stand beside bentwood café chairs in the middle of the dark hardwood floor. Fans spin overhead and light jazz fills the air as diners enjoy the cuisine.

Chef Greg Picolo creates a menu filled with mouth-watering dishes. Among the highlights
are Escargots Bourguignon, Roasted Eggplant and Coconut Soup, Sea Scallops with Wild
Mushroom Galette, Chocolate Crème Brulée and Lemon-Basil Sorbet.

Oysters, Spinach and Goat Cheese Beggars Purse with Apple-Smoked Bacon Vinaigrette

Drain oysters in a colander and reserve the juice. Sauté the oysters in 2 Tbsps. of butter with half of the onion and half of the garlic. Cook briefly until edges of oysters curl, then let cool.

Sauté the spinach in 4 Tbsps. of butter, with the remaining onions and garlic until barely wilted. Add the oyster juice, Pernod, nutmeg, salt and pepper and sauté until the spinach is cooked and has absorbed the liquid. Place in a colander to allow excess moisture to drain. Set aside and let the mixture cool.

Melt the remaining butter. Prepare the Phyllo by layering 4 sheets, each brushed with butter.

Place 2 Tbsps. of cooled spinach, four oysters and 1 Tbsp. of goat cheese in the center of the Phyllo. Bring ends of pastry up onto its center, like a purse, using additional butter to seal the pastry. Bake for 12 minutes at 375° until brown.

Cook bacon well, until very crispy. Remove bacon bits from pan and reserve on paper towel. Combine warm bacon oil with mustard, lemon juice, salt and black pepper in a mixer and blend to create an emulsion.

Place the hot beggar purse on a bed of mixed greens, drizzle with vinaigrette and garnish with the bacon bits.

Serves 8
Preparation Time:
  1 Hour
Preheat oven to 375°

- 32 oysters
- 1 lb. butter
- 1 lb. onion, minced fine
- 3 Tbsps. fresh garlic, chopped
- 2 lbs. fresh spinach, washed, stems removed
- 1 Tbsp. Pernod
- 1 tsp. nutmeg
  Salt and pepper to taste
- 32 Phyllo sheets
- 1 lb. goat cheese
- ¾ lb. apple-smoked bacon, diced
- 2 Tbsps. Creole or whole grain mustard
  Juice from 1 lemon

★

Crawfish and Mushroom Gumbo

Serves 4
Preparation Time:
  2 Hours

1½ cup light blond roux
     (½ cup of butter and
     1 cup of flour)
 5 onions, finely chopped
 3 celery stalks, finely
     chopped
 1 green bell pepper,
     finely chopped
 2 red bell peppers, finely
     chopped
 6 tsps. garlic, minced
     fine
 4 cups chicken stock
 2 cups reduced shrimp
     or crawfish stock
 1 cup veal demi-glaze
 3 lbs. crawfish tails
 2 cups Madeira wine
 3 lbs. shiitake
     mushrooms, chopped
     Salt and pepper to
     taste

P repare a roux by combining the butter and flour in a heavy saucepan. Cook over moderate heat until mixture turns light caramel color. Be sure to stir mixture constantly, as it can burn easily.

Add all the chopped vegetables to the roux. Sauté until tender. Add the garlic. With a wire whisk, slowly add the chicken and shrimp stocks, demi-glaze and wine to the roux and vegetable mixture until all stock is incorporated.

Cook for 45 minutes in saucepan, Sauté crawfish tails with mushrooms in a small amount of butter and oil. Add to stock mixture and let simmer for an additional 30 seconds.

Cooking Secret: Serve the Gumbo over rice, preferably pecan or wild rice.

Grilled Shrimps in a Creole Tomato Sauce with Andouille, Shiitake and Acorn Squash Orzo

Sauté ⅔ of the onions, bell pepper, celery and bay leaves until onions are clear, then add 1 Tbsp. of garlic, Worcestershire sauce, thyme and the tomatoes and cook for one hour. Add the lemon juice, adjust salt and pepper to taste and keep warm.

Cut acorn squash in half and remove the seeds. Sprinkle nutmeg and cinnamon over each half. Wrap in foil and bake at 350° for 1½ hours, until fork tender (do not overcook). Reserve until cool and cut the squash into a fine dice after removing the skin. Cut the Andouille sausage and sauté until lightly brown in butter. Add the remaining onions and garlic and sauté briefly before adding the sliced mushrooms. Deglaze with sherry, add the Orzo pasta, the chicken stock and cook like a risotto. When pasta is al dente, add the squash, adjust for salt and pepper to taste. Keep warm and reserve.

Before grilling the shrimps, marinate them in olive oil, salt, pepper and garlic.

Place the orzo in a ring mold or soup cup and place in the center of the plate. Display five shrimps per serving around the orzo and ladle the sauce over the shrimps.

Serves 8
Preparation Time:
 3 Hours
Preheat oven to 350°

- ½ cup olive oil
- 3 large yellow onions, minced
- 1 large green bell pepper, minced
- 2 ribs of celery, minced
- 4 fresh bay leaves
- 4 Tbsps. garlic, minced
- 3 Tbsps. Worcestershire sauce
- ¼ Tbsp. fresh thyme leaves
- 5 lbs. peeled tomatoes
- Juice from 1 lemon
- Salt and pepper to taste
- 1 acorn squash
- ½ Tbsp. cinnamon
- ½ Tbsp. nutmeg
- 1 lb. Andouille sausage
- 6 Tbsps. butter
- 1½ lbs. shiitake mushrooms, stems removed, sliced
- ½ cup dry sherry
- 1 lb. Orzo pasta
- 2 cups low salt chicken stock
- 40 U-12 shrimps (5 per person)

☆

Almond and Sun-Dried Cranberry Bread Pudding with a Spiced Brandy Crème Anglaise

Serves 8
Preparation Time:
  1¾ Hours
(note marinating time)

  1 **cup sun-dried**
     cranberries
  1 **cup brandy**
  1 **loaf of French bread,**
     10 oz.
  4 **cups milk**
  2 **cups sugar**
  8 **Tbsps. melted butter**
  4 **eggs**
  2 **Tbsps. pure vanilla**
     extract
  1 **cup shredded coconut**
  1 **cup slivered almonds,**
     toasted, chopped
  1 **Tbsp. nutmeg**

Crème Anglaise:
  6 **egg yolks**
  ½ **cup brandy**
  ½ **cup sugar**
  1 **tsp. cinnamon**
  2 **cups heavy cream**

P lace the cranberries in a bowl with ½ cup of brandy and marinate for one hour to plump the fruit.

Combine the remaining ingredients in a bowl with the drained cranberries. Pour the mixture (moist but not too soggy) into a 9 × 12-inch baking dish and bake at 350° in a non-preheated oven for 1¼ hours.

For the crème anglaise: In a double boiler, combine yolks, brandy, sugar and cinnamon. Cook until mixture has thickened. Add the cream and cook until the mixture coats the back of a spoon. Serve warm over the pudding.

☆

Roasted Banana and Yam Sorbet

Roast the yams and bananas until soft and dark. Meanwhile, in a saucepan, make a syrup by mixing the sugar, water, pineapple juice, lemon juice and pectin. Boil sauce for 2 minutes.

In a large mixing bowl, blend together the bananas and yams. Add the syrup, mixing until smooth. Strain through a chinois or sieve and add the vanilla.

Process in an ice cream machine.

Serves 4
Preparation Time:
  50 Minutes
(note freezing time)
Preheat oven to 450°

  1 lb. yams
  1 lb. bananas
  ¾ cup sugar
  1 cup water
  ½ cup unsweetened
     pineapple juice
     Juice from 1 lemon
1¼ tsps. pectin
  ½ tsp. vanilla

LE JARDIN SUR LE BAYOU

Le Jardin Sur Le Bayou
256 Lower Country Drive
Bourg, Louisiana 70343
(504) 594-2722
ROOM RATES: $85, including a gourmet breakfast

E njoy Cajun hospitality on this 26-acre registered wildlife sanctuary, featuring century-old live oaks and native plants teeming with hummingbirds and butterflies. Stroll quiet garden paths under an oak canopy, pause at bridges and enjoy goldfish ponds, a swing or just sitting on a garden bench and watching the extensive variety of birds.

A comfortable and tastefully decorated private upstairs suite, set back from a quiet country road, offers central air and heat, cable TV, telephone, refrigerator, use of screened breezeway and laundry facilities. Owners and innkeepers Dave and Jo Ann Cognet create magical breakfasts each morning, served in the garden or dining area overlooking the fish ponds.

This highly recommended bed and breakfast inn is just one hour from New Orleans. Consider staying at least two nights to enjoy the home cooking and garden tour.

Fresh Cherry Muffins

I n a large mixing bowl, cream the butter, then add the sugar and beat until light and lemon colored. Beat in the eggs.

Sift together the dry ingredients and add to the butter mixture beginning and ending with 1 Tbsp. milk.

Stir in the cherry halves, pecans and almond extract.

Bake in paper-lined muffin tins in a 375° oven for 15 to 20 minutes. If making mini loaves, adjust the time accordingly, about 25 to 30 minutes.

Cooking Secret: This recipe, developed by Kathy Holt, is delicious right out of the oven. Make plenty—they also freeze well.

Yield:
  12 to 16 large muffins
  or 4 mini loaves.
Preparation Time:
  45 Minutes
Preheat oven to 375°

  ½ **cup butter or**
    margarine
  1 **cup sugar**
  2 **eggs**
  2 **cups all-purpose flour**
  ½ **tsp. salt**
  ½ **tsp. baking soda**
  1 **Tbsp. double-acting**
    baking powder
  2 **Tbsps. buttermilk or**
    sour milk
  1 **cup fresh or frozen**
    cherry halves (pitted)
  ¾ **cup chopped pecans**
  2 **tsps. almond extract**

★

LOYD HALL PLANTATION

Loyd Hall Plantation
292 Loyd Bridge Road
Cheneyville, Louisiana 71325
(800) 240-8135
(318) 776-5641
ROOM RATES: $95–$125

Situated on the banks of Bayou Boeuf, Loyd Hall Plantation's colorful past is marked by countless tales of survival throughout its 175-year history. This 640-acre plantation, in continuous operation since 1800, provides guests with a hands-on look at Louisiana agriculture, with crops of corn, cotton, soybeans and cattle. A few personal friends, like Clarence the donkey, will steal your heart. And the mysterious spirit of a violin player who appears at midnight on the second-floor verandah is one you'll always remember.

Loyd Hall features ornate plaster ceilings, suspended staircases and rare antiques. Charming and private bed and breakfast accommodations are truly one-of-a-kind.

Hot Artichoke Dip

Mix all ingredients thoroughly with mixer except the artichoke hearts. Fold in the artichokes.

Pour into pumpernickel loaf. Cover and bake for
1 hour at 350° or until heated thoroughly.

Serve hot with crackers, assorted breads or chips.

Serves 6 to 8
Preparation Time:
  30 Minutes
Preheat oven to 350°

    1 stick butter
    1 cup sour cream
    1 cup black olives, sliced
    8 oz. cream cheese
    1½ cups cheddar cheese,
      grated
    1 cup green onions,
      chopped
      White pepper to taste
      Tabasco to taste
      Artichoke hearts,
      drained, rinsed,
      quartered
    1 round or oval
      pumpernickel loaf,
      hollowed out

☆

WINDSOR COURT HOTEL

Windsor Court Hotel
300 Gravier Street
New Orleans, Louisiana 70130
(800) 262-2662
(504) 523-6000
ROOM RATES: $250–$650

I n the center of New Orleans' business district, only four blocks from its famous French Quarter, stands this gracious, award-winning contemporary hotel. Furnished and decorated throughout in traditional style, the elegant decor is complemented by European arts and antiques, including works by Reynolds, Gainsborough and Huysman.

All deluxe guest rooms have a dressing room adjoining the bedroom and bathroom, television, soundproofed walls and top-of-the-line safety measures including smoke detectors and sprinklers. The suites offer a separate living room, a compact kitchen and bay windows overlooking the Mississippi River or the city of New Orleans.

Dining at the Windsor Court Hotel has quickly attracted the attention of those who appreciate fine food and wine, offering a choice of menus, complemented by impeccable service. Executive Chef Jeff Tunks creates an international menu that has made him one of "the best of the best." The wine cellar is one of the finest in the United States.

Macadamia Nut Crusted Halibut with Mango Lime Sauce

In a saucepan over low heat, combine the mango with the white wine and honey. Reduce to ¼ liquid. Add the cream and reduce further. Place in a blender and purée. Strain. Season with salt and lime juice. Reserve.

Mix the bread crumbs and macadamia nuts in a bowl.

Dip the halibut in the egg and then dip in the bread crumb-macadamia nut mixture. Pan sauté in olive oil until golden brown. Finish in the oven for 3 to 5 minutes.

In sesame oil stir fry the black sesame seeds.

Place a pool of the mango sauce on a plate and top with the halibut. Garnish with snow peas, black sesame seeds and lime wedges.

Serves 4
Preparation Time:
  45 Minutes
Preheat oven to 350°

- 2 mangos, skinned, seeded
- ¾ cup white wine
- 2 Tbsps. honey
- 1 cup cream
- 1 cup fresh bread crumbs
- ½ cup macadamia nuts, chopped
- 2 lbs. halibut
- 4 eggs, beaten
- 4 Tbsps. olive oil
- 1 Tbsp. sesame oil
- 1 tsp. black sesame seeds
- ⅓ lb. snow peas, steamed
- 2 lime wedges, garnish

MISSISSIPPI: The Magnolia State

Sometimes it's easy to overlook Mississippi, sandwiched as it is between Alabama, Louisiana, Tennessee and Arkansas. The largest of its cities, Jackson, has fewer than 200,000 inhabitants. And its land, either poorly drained, flat bottomland of the Mississippi River, or gently rolling hills that climb all the way up to the highest point in the state, Woodall Mountain, 806 feet above sea level, hardly make it a place of high geographical drama. But if you skip over this state on your travels, you'll certainly miss an important chunk of United States history—and you'll miss the home state of many whose beginnings have cast giant shadows across the cultural stage of the entire nation.

The early history of Mississippi is similar to that of its neighbors. The Spanish were the first Europeans to spot the place and the French were the first to establish a permanent settlement at Ocean Springs in 1699. But the population influx did not begin until 1763, when France ceded the area to Great Britain and settlers migrated here from Virginia, Georgia and the Carolinas. The Territory of Mississippi was established in 1798, and it was the 20th state to enter the Union (1817).

Located as it was and dependent on cotton and the slavery necessary to perpetuate its way of life, Mississippi was the second state to secede from the Union. One of the longest sieges of the war, the 47-day Battle of Vicksburg, ended when the town fell to General Ulysses S. Grant. The war's end brought the worst of all possible times to this bastion of Southern gentility. Only one out of every four soldiers Mississippi sent into battle returned, and Reconstruction was particularly harsh. The state remained an agricultural backwater—the poorest in the nation—until the mid-1960s.

But if the state suffered, it produced far more than its share of men and women who gave voice to its sorrow and vigor to its renewed spirit. Among them were Dana Andrews, Jimmy Buffet, Hodding Carter III, William Faulkner, Shelby Foote, John Grisham, Jim Henson, James Earl Jones, B.B. King, Elvis Presley, Leontyne Price, Charlie Pride, Eudora Welty, Tennessee Williams, Oprah Winfrey, Richard Wright and Tammy Wynette.

Today, Mississippi is one of the nation's largest producers of upholstered furniture. Agriculture remains a significant focus of the state's economy, and recent successful experiments in the pond raising of catfish and the production of fryer chickens have brought new wealth to the state. Mississippi is very much a part of the Space Age: all of the main-stage engine test firings are performed at the John C. Stennis Space Center near Picayune. Advanced solid-fuel rocket motors are manufactured at the NASA/Lockheed-Aerojet plant in northeast Mississippi. And with its abundant rainfall and gentle climate, the state's Gulf Coast, with its plethora of casinos, has become a magnet for tourism.

Here are some highlights of a trip to Mississippi.

CASINOS, for those so disposed, which feature both gambling and entertainment, may be found throughout Mississippi, primarily at Biloxi (BOOMTOWN, CASINO MAGIC, GRAND CASINO, ISLE OF CAPRI CASINO), Clermont Harbor (BAYOU CADDY'S JUBILEE CASINO), Gulfport (COPA CASINO, GRAND CASINO GULFPORT), Lula (LADY LUCK RHYTHM AND BLUES CASINO), Philadelphia (SILVER STAR CASINO), Robinsonville (BALLY'S SALOON AND GAMBLING HALL, CIRCUS CIRCUS CASINO, HARRAH'S TUNICA CASINO, SAM'S TOWN GAMBLING HALL, SHERATON CASINO) and Vicksburg (HARRAH'S CASINO, ISLE OF CAPRI, RAINBOW CASINO).

The Beauvoir-Jefferson Davis Shrine in Biloxi

Photo from the
Mississippi Department of Archives and History

The Beauvoir-Jefferson Davis Shrine in **BILOXI,** the last home of the president of the Confederate States of America, houses a substantial Confederate Museum in the Confederate Veterans' Hospital Building: there's a proliferation of Civil War guns, uniforms, flags, medical instruments and personal belongings. A nearby cemetery contains more than 700 Confederate gravestones. The city itself is a delightful coastal resort, combining the charm of the Old South with 21st century, high-tech gambling casinos.

Stop in **GREENVILLE** and spend at least two hours visiting the re-created ante-bellum FLOREWOOD RIVER PLANTATION. Costumed guides take you through the main buildings and the outbuildings and you find yourself in the midst of 1850s Mississippi. You can pick cotton in the late summer. The guides will show you demonstrations of period crafts. The first Saturday of November marks a Civil War re-enactment and there's a Christmas candlelight tour the first Saturday in December.

An old-time wedding anniversary party

Photo from the
Mississippi Department of Archives and History

The **GULF ISLANDS NATIONAL SEASHORE** stretches from Fort Walton Beach, Florida, to Gulfport, Mississippi. The long, narrow islands are moving westward each year, and shifting sand dunes add or subtract from the area of each. Ship Island, accessible by excursion boats, was a staging ground for the British in the War of 1812. Fort Massachusetts, a Union fortress during the Civil War, is one of several coastal defense facilities dating from the 19th century.

A trading post called LeFleur's Bluff became today's capital of **JACKSON**. With a population of nearly 197,000, it is the largest city in the state. Originally named for Andrew Jackson, it earned a much sadder name, "Chimneyville," when General William Tecumseh Sherman burned it to the ground in 1863. Some notable buildings, among them the GOVERNOR'S MANSION (1842), survived, among other things because it served as Grant's and Sherman's headquarters during the Civil War. A 39-acre complex tracing the economic and technological progress of the state may be found at the MISSISSIPPI AGRICULTURE AND FORESTRY/NATIONAL AGRICULTURAL AVIATION MUSEUM next to Smith-Wills Stadium.

The city of **MERIDIAN** honors its native son, Jimmie Rodgers, with a full-week festival the last week of May. The JIMMIE RODGERS MEMORIAL AND MUSEUM is located 2 miles northwest of the city.

The JOHN C. STENNIS SPACE CENTER, a 13,500-acre installation, is a center for space, environmental and oceanographic research and study. On a tour of the facility, you'll see a moon rock, an Apollo command module, numerous exhibits and active testing of space shuttle main engines. It's located near **PICAYUNE,** which was named by a lady whose husband ran a newspaper in New Orleans that sold for a half-dime, or "picayune."

ROWAN OAK in **OXFORD** is a white clapboard house where Nobel prize-winning author William Faulkner wrote most of his works. Built in 1844, Faulkner purchased the house in 1930 and restored it. Today, it's preserved to look exactly as it did at the time of Faulkner's death in 1962.

You can't stop in **TUPELO** without visiting a much smaller white-frame house. Take the Veteran's Boulevard, exit off US Highway 78 or the Main Street exit off US Highway 45 and follow the signs to the ELVIS PRESLEY CENTER AND MUSEUM, where "The King" was born. There's a memorial chapel, as well as a museum with Presley artifacts and a 15-acre park.

The **VICKSBURG NATIONAL MILITARY PARK,** 1,700 acres adjoining the city of Vicksburg, was the site of the most significant Civil War battle to take place in Mississippi. Forts, trenches and artillery positions have been recreated on authentic sites. More than 1,250 memorials, statues and monuments honor the Confederate soldiers who died here.

LIZA'S

Liza's
NOUVELLE CUISINE
657 South Canal Street
Natchez, Mississippi
(601) 446-6368
Dinner Tuesday–Sunday 5:30PM–10PM
AVERAGE DINNER FOR TWO: $55

Debuting in a historical building in 1993, Liza's quickly become a favorite in Natchez. Known for its Nouvelle Cuisine, with influences from the Southwest and Creole cooking, the eatery invites diners to feast on fresh seafood, veal, beef and vegetarian dishes. Chef Terranova is known for using fresh herbs and a savory variety of sauces.

The restaurant is comprised of five dining rooms in the renovated, two-story house. The use of whites and off-whites in the decor gives the rooms a light and spacious feel.

Liza's menu changes about once a month, but in the past has featured such dishes as Fresh Crawfish Tails over Linguine in Garlic-Chive Sauce, Parmesan-Crusted Scaloppini of Veal and Pan-Fried Catfish with Louisiana Hot Sauce Beurre Blanc Served with Parmesan Garlic Grits and Black-Eyed Pea Relish, which is far more gourmet than it sounds. The wine list is constantly improving.

LIZA'S MENU FOR FOUR

Grilled Gulf Shrimp with Louisiana Hot Sauce Beurre Blanc

Corn and Lima Bean Ragout

Seared Marinated Pork Tenderloin

Creamed Sweet Potatoes and Stir-Fried Collard Greens

Pecan Tart

Grilled Gulf Shrimp with Corn and Lima Bean Ragout and Louisiana Hot Sauce Beurre Blanc

Sauté onions over medium heat in olive oil for 2 minutes. Add the garlic, corn and lima beans. Sauté for 5 minutes, stirring frequently. Add the chicken broth (if using canned broth, reduce or eliminate the salt) and simmer until broth is completely reduced.

Remove from heat and whisk in the butter. Season to taste. Keep warm.

Grill the shrimp or sear in a hot skillet with a small amount of oil, about 1½ minutes per side, until done.

To serve, place the ragout in the center of individual serving plates. Place 3 cooked shrimp around the ragout. Ladle the sauce (recipe follows) around and over the shrimp.

Serves 4
Preparation Time:
  25 Minutes

¼ cup red onion, diced
1 Tbsp. olive oil
2 tsps. garlic, minced
4 ears of corn, kernels cut from the cob
1½ cups lima beans, frozen
2 cups chicken broth, fresh or canned
2 Tbsps. butter
   Salt and pepper to taste
12 large shrimp, 16/20 count, peeled, deveined
   Salt and cayenne pepper to taste
   Louisiana Hot Sauce Beurre Blanc (recipe follows)

☆

Louisiana Hot Sauce Beurre Blanc

Preparation Time:
 10 Minutes

 ½ **cup white wine**
 2 **Tbsps. lemon juice**
 1 **bay leaf**
 1 **shallot, minced**
 ¼ **cup heavy cream**
 1 **tsp. Louisiana hot**
 sauce
 ½ **lb. butter, cubed**

lace the wine, lemon juice, bay leaf and shallot in a saucepan. Bring to a boil, then lower heat and simmer until reduced by half.
Add the cream and hot sauce and reduce by ¾.
Remove from heat and whisk in the butter. Keep warm.

☆

Seared Marinated Pork Tenderloin

or the marinade, mix together the teriyaki sauce, ginger, garlic, sugar, water, sesame oil and cilantro in a nonreactive dish.

Trim the tenderloins and marinate for 30 minutes to 1 hour.

Remove the pork from the marinade. Season with salt and pepper.

Pour the olive oil into a skillet and heat until very hot. Add the pork (be sure pork is dry or it will flare up) and sear on all sides for about 8 minutes. Remove from heat and keep warm.

To serve, place a serving of sweet potatoes (recipe follows) in the center of the plate. Slice each tenderloin into three pieces and place around the potatoes. Place greens (recipe follows) on the plate between the pieces of pork.

Serves 4
Preparation Time:
  20 Minutes
(note marinating time)

2 cups teriyaki sauce
2 Tbsps. ginger, minced
2 Tbsps. garlic, minced
½ cup sugar
1 cup water
2 Tbsps. sesame oil
4 Tbsps. cilantro,
    chopped
4 pork tenderloins,
    trimmed
    Salt and pepper
2 Tbsps. olive oil

☆

Stir Fried Collard Greens and Creamed Sweet Potatoes

Serves 6
Preparation Time:
 25 Minutes
(note cooling time)
Preheat oven to 350°

12 large sweet potatoes
 1 cup heavy cream
 1 tsp. cinnamon, ground
 ½ tsp. cayenne pepper
    Salt to taste
 6 pieces bacon, diced
 ½ cup onion, diced
 4 bunches collard
    greens, stems
    removed, julienned
    fine
 4 Tbsps. cider vinegar
    Pepper to taste

Bake the sweet potatoes in a 350° oven until soft. Allow to cool, then peel and put the pulp into a saucepan. Add the cream and seasonings and bring to a boil. Remove from heat and whisk the potato mixture with a wire whip to a mashed consistency. Keep warm.

In a large skillet over medium heat, render the bacon with the onions until bacon is crisp. Turn up the heat, adding the greens and tossing the pan until the greens wilt. Add the vinegar and toss with salt and pepper to taste. Remove from heat.

Pecan Tart

Prebake the pie crust in a 9-inch tart shell in a 350° oven for 10 minutes. Remove from the oven.

With a mixer blend together the dark and light corn syrups, vanilla extract and cinnamon until everything comes together, but do not over mix.

Turn the mixer to low and add the eggs, three at a time. Combine until the mixture comes together. Add the butter all at once, beating for 30 seconds. Set aside.

Fill the crust with pecans and pour the syrup-egg mixture over them to the top of the tart pan. Place on a cookie sheet and bake in 350° oven for 20 to 30 minutes.

The tart should be soft in the middle, but not runny. Allow to cool completely before cutting.

Serve with whipped cream or ice cream.

Yield:
  One 9-inch Tart
Preparation Time:
  15 Minutes
Cooking Time:
  30 Minutes
Preheat oven to 350°

  1 pie crust
2½ cups dark corn syrup
  ½ cup light corn syrup
  ¼ Tbsp. vanilla extract
  ¼ tsp. ground cinnamon
  9 eggs
  ⅓ cup melted butter
1½ cups pecans
    Whipped cream or ice cream, optional

NICK'S

Nick's
ECLECTIC FINE CUISINE
1501 Lakeland Drive
Jackson, Mississippi
(601) 981-8017
Lunch Monday–Friday 11AM–2PM
Dinner Monday–Thursday 6PM–10PM
Dinner Friday and Saturday 6PM–10:30PM
Closed Sunday
AVERAGE DINNER FOR TWO: $60

Chef/owner Nick Apostle opened Nick's in 1983 and from the start it has been a star on the Jackson restaurant scene. Nick's is open all afternoon and the lounge prides the best place in the city to relax and enjoy a glass of vino in anticipation of a fine meal. Bring a hefty appetite with you because Nick's gives you a lot of food.

Nick's boasts one of the best (some say the best) wine list in the area.

Your best bets for dinner are the Lobster Bisque, Veal Piccata, Char-Grilled Beef Tenderloin, Southwestern Grilled Chicken Breast and Raspberry Sorbet.

NICK'S MENU FOR FOUR

Pan-Fried Soft-Shell Crab with a Shrimp and Crab Meat Butter Cream Sauce

Scalloped Potatoes with Sweet Marjoram and Parmesan Cheese

Pan-Fried Soft-Shell Crab with a Shrimp and Crab Meat Butter Cream Sauce

In a large bowl combine the salt, onion powder, paprika, cayenne, white pepper, garlic powder, glack pepper, oregano and thyme. Mix all ingredients together for the seasoning mix and set aside.

Beat together the milk and egg in a pan until well blended.

In a separate pan, add 1 Tbsp. seasoning mix to the flour and mix well. Sprinkle a Tbsp. of the remaining seasoning mix lightly on both sides of each crab. Dredge each crab in the seasoned flour, shaking off excess. Soak in the egg-milk mixture and drain off excess.

Heat about ½ to ¾-inch vegetable oil in a very large heavy skillet to about 350°. Fry the crabs, shell down in the hot oil for 2 to 3 minutes or until golden brown.

Drain on paper towels. Serve immediately with the shrimp and crabmeat butter cream sauce.

Cooking Secret: You cannot reserve the crabs once they are cooked as the crust will get tacky and the crabs will lose their natural moisture and deflate.

Serves 4
Preparation Time:
  30 Minutes

  1 **Tbsp. salt**
  1 **tsp. onion powder**
  1 **tsp. sweet Hungarian**
    paprika
  ¼ **tsp. cayenne**
  ½ **tsp. white pepper**
  ½ **tsp. garlic powder**
  ¼ **tsp. black pepper**
  ¼ **tsp. dried oregano**
    leaves
  ¼ **tsp. dried thyme leaves**
  1 **cup milk**
  2 **eggs, beaten**
  2 **cups all-purpose flour**
  6 **jumbo soft-shell crabs,**
    cleaned
    Vegetable oil for pan
    frying
    Shrimp and crab meat
    butter cream sauce
    (recipe follows)

☆

Shrimp and Crab Meat Butter Cream Sauce

Serves 4
Preparation Time:
  30 Minutes

1½ cups shrimp or seafood
    stock
½ lb. unsalted butter
⅓ cup green onions,
    thinly sliced
3 tsps. flour
1 cup heavy cream
½ tsp. salt
⅛ tsp. cayenne pepper
¾ lb. medium-sized
    shrimp, peeled (about
    2 dozen)
½ lb. jumbo lump crab
    meat, picked clean for
    shells

Bring the stock to a boil in a 2-qt. saucepan then reduce to a very slow simmer.

While the stock is coming to a boil in another saucepan, melt the butter with the green onions over medium heat. Sauté for about 1 minute. Add the flour and blend with a metal whisk until smooth. Reduce heat to low and continue cooking and whisking constantly for one minute. Do not let it brown.

Pour the simmering stock into the butter-flour mixture over low heat, whisking till smooth. Gradually add the cream, whisking constantly, then add the salt and cayenne pepper.

Stir in the shrimp and crabmeat. Continue cooking just until the shrimp are pink and plump, about 2 to 4 minutes, stirring gently. Keep warm and set aside.

Scalloped Potatoes with Sweet Marjoram and Parmesan Cheese

Butter a 6-cup grating dish or shallow casserole. Layer ⅕ of the potato slices in the gratin dish and season with ¼ each of the salt, pepper, nutmeg, garlic, marjoram and Parmesan cheese. Repeat the layering 3 times. Top with a final layer of potato slices, overlapping them attractively.

Combine the cream with ½ cup of water and pour evenly over the potatoes.

Cover the dish with aluminum foil. Bake at 350° for 1½ hours, then uncover and bake for 30 minutes longer or until slightly browned. Remove from the oven and let stand 10 minutes before serving.

Serves 4
Preparation Time:
  2 Hours
Preheat oven to 350°

  4 **large baking potatoes, peeled, thinly sliced**
  1 **tsp. salt**
  ¼ **tsp. freshly ground pepper**
  ¼ **tsp. freshly grated nutmeg**
  2 **garlic cloves, minced**
  1 **Tbsp. dried sweet marjoram or ¼ cup fresh, chopped**
  ¼ **cup Parmesan cheese, grated**
  2 **cups heavy cream**
  ½ **cup water**

☆

THE PALETTE RESTAURANT AT THE MISSISSIPPI MUSEUM OF ART

The Palette Restaurant at the Mississippi Museum of Art
AMERICAN ETHNIC CUISINE
201 East Pascagoula Street
Jackson, Mississippi
(601) 960-1515
Lunch 11:30AM–1:30PM
Dinners by Special Arrangement
AVERAGE MEAL FOR TWO: $25

T he culinary arts and the visual arts come together at The Palette Restaurant at the Mississippi Museum of Art. Located in the upper atrium gallery of the museum, the artistic eatery offers an intriguing atmosphere and a refreshing menu selection, ranging from catch of the day and fresh pasta dishes to salads and sandwiches. When the weather is nice, the balcony is open for dining.

Exhibitions rotate frequently in the atrium gallery so diners may enjoy a variety of visual art displays. Live music is provided daily by museum volunteer pianists. Waiters and cashiers are museum volunteers as well.

Chef Christopher Haddad's menu includes such creations as the Starving Artist (cup of soup, cheese, fruit and crusty French bread), Pasta Puttanesca, Vegetarian Grilled Eggplant Sandwich and Wine Country Pie (layers of meats, cheeses and vegetables).

THE PALETTE'S MENU FOR EIGHT

Wine Country Pie

Wine Country Pie

In a large mixing bowl, stir the flour and salt together. Cut in the shortening until blended well. Add the ice water a little at a time until you form a good paste. Refrigerate until needed.

In a separate mixing bowl, combine the ricotta, mozzarella and Parmesan cheeses, eggs and spinach. Mix well and set aside.

In a sauté pan, lightly sauté the fennel, shallots and garlic until semi-translucent. Set aside.

Roll out the pie dough and line a 14-inch springform pan. Reserve part of the dough for the top.

Spoon in a layer of the sautéed vegetables. Then cover the vegetables with salami. Top with the cheese mixture. Cover with red pepper slices and top with the remaining crust.

Bake at 350° for 1 hour or until golden brown. Let the pie sit for 45 minutes before cutting.

Cooking Secret: Serve with fresh fruit and your favorite wine.

Yield:
  1 Pie
Preparation Time:
  1¼ Hours
Preheat oven to 350°

- 4 cups flour
- 1 tsp. salt
- 1½ cups shortening
  Ice water as needed
- 1 cup ricotta cheese
- 1 cup mozzarella cheese, shredded
- 1 cup Parmesan cheese, grated
- 4 eggs, beaten
- 1 cup fresh spinach, chopped
- 1 large fennel bulb, chopped
- 4 shallots, peeled, chopped
- 3 garlic cloves, minced
- 1 cup salami, diced
- 1 red bell pepper, roasted

MILLSAPS BUIE HOUSE

Millsaps Buie House
628 North State Street
Jackson, Mississippi 39202
(800) 784-0221
(601) 352-0221
ROOM RATES: $85–$170

This Victorian, Queen Anne-style house, built in 1888, was constructed for Major Reuben Webster Millsaps, founder of the Methodist college in Jackson.

Since the inn is in the heart of historical Jackson, history buffs will likely want to visit the nearby War Memorial Building, Old Capitol Museum and the Mississippi Museum of Natural Science.

Many of the rooms bear the traditional architecture of 14-foot ceilings, hand-molded frieze work, rich mahogany woodwork and bay windows.

Understated elegance is the only way to describe the inn, with its blend of French, English and Victorian pieces and reproductions. Each of the 11 bedrooms is exquisitely furnished with antiques and period pieces. The soft color scheme of roses, blues and creams soothes weary travelers. Every room has a private bath, cable television and telephone.

Guests may relax in the drawing room, library or parlor while enjoying Southern hospitality at its best.

Bran Muffins

I n a large mixing bowl, pour the boiling water over the All-Bran cereal and bran flakes. Add the sugar, short-ening, eggs, buttermilk, flour, soda and salt. Stir until well combined.

Bake in greased muffin tins at 375° for 15 to 20 minutes.

Cooking Secret: This batter keeps well in the refrigerator for up to two weeks, so you can make fresh muffins every day.

Yield:
  72 muffins
Preparation Time:
  15 Minutes
Preheat oven to 375°

2 cups boiling water
4 cups All-Bran cereal
2 cups 100% bran flakes
3 cups sugar
1 cup + 2 Tbsps.
  shortening
4 eggs, beaten
1 qt. buttermilk
5 cups plain flour
5 tsps. soda
1 tsp. salt

MONMOUTH PLANTATION

Monmouth Plantation
36 Melrose
Natchez, Mississippi 39120
(800) 828-4531
(601) 446-5852
ROOM RATES: $120–$225

As you wander the lush grounds of magnificent Monmouth Plantation, you enter the dreams of two men. The first, John Anthony Quitman, was an American war hero and prominent politician who owned the mansion in the decades before the Civil War. The second man created the soul behind Monmouth today—Ron Riches, a businessman with a love for history and a fascination with the ante-bellum South.

Monmouth Plantation has been consistently ranked one of the country's most romantic inns. Restored to its pre-Civil War splendor, the inn integrates period art and furnishings with modern comforts. The surrounding 26 acres of manicured gardens abound with magnolias and moss-draped oak trees.

Guests have a choice of 27 rooms and suites. The inn enfolds guests in luxury with attentive service, complimentary Southern breakfasts and sumptuous five-course dinners.

Quail with Plum Sauce

Prepare the marinade by combining the garlic, pepper, oil and wine in a mixing bowl. Pour the marinade over the quail and marinate for 20 minutes.

Remove from marinade and grill or pan fry in just enough olive oil to coat skillet for approximately 8 minutes per side.

For the sauce: Drain the plums and save juice.

Pour the plums in a blender and purée.

In a sauté pan, melt butter and gently sauté the onions until golden brown. Add the plum purée, plum juice and remaining ingredients and simmer for 30 minutes, or until the sauce has thickened.

Serves 6
Preparation Time:
  1 Hour
(note marinating time)

Quail:
  1 garlic clove, crushed
  1 Tbsp. black pepper
  ¼ cup oil
  1¼ cups red wine
  12 quail

Sauce:
  1 lb. purple plums, fresh
    or canned
  ¼ cup butter
  3 Tbsps. onions, chopped
  ¼ cup fresh lemon juice
  ¼ cup brown sugar
  2 Tbsps. bottled chili
    sauce
  1 tsp. Worcestershire
    sauce
  ½ tsp. ground ginger

☆

OAK SQUARE PLANTATION

Oak Square Plantation
1207 Church Street
Port Gibson, Mississippi 39150
(800) 729-0240
(601) 437-4350
ROOM RATES: $85–$125

O ak Square, Port Gibson's largest and most palatial mansion, was once the home of a cotton planter. Originally built circa 1850, it is on the National Register of Historic Places and in Mississippi's First National Historic District. Beautiful grounds with courtyard, fountain and gazebo are a fitting complement to this impressive home, which exemplifies the grandeur of ante-bellum days and houses many fine period antiques.

Six fluted Corinthian columns, each 22 feet tall, welcome guests. This Greek revival-style mansion is comprised of the main house, two guest houses, a carriage house and quarters. Guests receive a tour of the inn, which reveals family heirloom antiques, ornate mill-work, spectacular chandeliers and a massive divided staircase leading to an unusual minstrel gallery. A rare collection of Civil War memorabilia belonging to the owner's great-grandfather is on display throughout the house.

Each luxurious guest room is furnished with period antiques, elegantly draped canopied beds and private baths with vanities.

Sweet Potato Pone

Peel and slice the potatoes and boil until soft. Drain and mash the potatoes until smooth. Stir in the margarine or butter until melted.

Add the remaining ingredients and stir until well blended.

Bake in an uncovered baking dish at 350° for about 45 minutes to 1 hour for a deep dish; or about 15 minutes less for a shallow dish. Serve hot or chilled.

Cooking Secret: For sweet potato pie, pour mixture into a pastry pie shell and bake at 350° for about 30 minutes.

Serves 8
Preparation Time:
   15 Minutes
Cooking Time:
   1 Hour
Preheat oven to 350°

   4 medium sweet
      potatoes
   1 stick margarine or
      butter
1½ cups sugar
   2 large eggs
   2 Tbsps. vanilla extract
   2 Tbsps. almond extract
   2 Tbsps. corn starch
   ¼ cup milk
   2 tsps. lemon juice or
      ¼ tsp. lemon extract
      Cinnamon to taste

☆

NORTH CAROLINA: The Tarheel State

Although North Carolinians had strong British ties, the colony chafed under British rule. On May 20, 1775, the citizens of Mecklenburg County (Charlotte) declared their independence from England—more than a year before the official Declaration of Independence set the stage for the Revolutionary War. North Carolina entered the Union as the 12th of the original 13 states in 1789.

Postwar North Carolina was plagued by poverty, ineffectual government, economic depression and the slavery issue. Although it believed in the preservation of the Union, it reluctantly seceded in May 1861. Following the Civil War, North Carolina, which had supplied more troops than any other state, and whose losses made up more than one-fourth of the Confederate Army's total casualties, was devastated. The prostrate state was further pillaged by rapacious carpetbaggers.

Until the 1960s, North Carolina tried everything within its power to enforce white supremacy. Despite a troubled history, North Carolina has achieved a great deal. The University of North Carolina, the first state university in the country, was established at Chapel Hill in 1795, and today the state is home to Duke University, Wake Forest and North Carolina State, all nationally respected institutions of higher learning.

North Carolina is known for tobacco, furniture and textiles. People from all over the country come here to purchase high quality furniture for their homes at savings so substantial that they pay for their journey and then some. Tobacco companies, faced with ever-increasing pressure from anti-tobacconists, attempt—not always successfully—to find protection in the North Carolina courts. Although North Carolina produces two-thirds of the nation's bright leaf tobacco, farmers are increasingly uncertain about their future and are turning to more diversified crops, such as corn, cotton, soybeans and peanuts.

North Carolina's climate is as varied as its terrain: subtropical in southeast, medium-continental in mountain region, and tempered by the Gulf Stream and the mountains in the West. The Blue Ridge and Appalachian Mountains—among the oldest landforms in America, converge: there are more than forty mountains higher than 6,000 feet, including Mount Mitchell, at 6,684 feet the highest point in the Eastern United States.

☆

Famous North Carolinians include Richard J. Gatling (the Gatling gun), Billy Graham, Andy Griffith, Presidents Andrew Jackson, Andrew Johnson and James K. Polk, Michael Jordan, Charles Kuralt, Dolley Madison, Edward R. Murrow, Enos Slaughter and Thomas Wolfe.

Here are some highlights of a trip to the Tarheel State.

The **BILTMORE ESTATE** near Asheville, is the largest home in America. George Washington Vanderbilt, grandson of railroad magnate Cornelius Vanderbilt, opened the doors of his 250-room French Renaissance chateau a century ago. The home features labor-saving devices that did not come into general use until many years later: clothes washers and dryers,

The Biltmore Estate

an electric rotary spit, electric dumbwaiters, central heating, plumbing and electric lights throughout. The main residence occupies four acres of floorspace, with 43 bathtubs, 65 fireplaces and 1,354 windows. Priceless art (Renoir, John Singer Sargent, Albrecht Dürer, James McNeil Whistler) adorns the walls; the rooms are filled with antique Chippendale furniture; you'll find the chess table that Napoleon Bonaparte took with him to St. Helena and many pieces of Ming Dynasty China within the house. The 8,000 acre spread includes 75 acres of formal gardens, The Walled Garden which has 50,000 Dutch tulips in the spring, the Rose Garden with 2,000 plants, and the 21-acre Azalea Garden surround the house.

At **MOUNT MITCHELL STATE PARK,** near Asheville, you'll savor dramatic sights from the highest summit in the Eastern U.S. The mountain was named for Dr. Elisha Mitchell, who fell to his death while attempting to measure the mountain's altitude. While in the area, drive over a portion of the

☆

BLUE RIDGE PARKWAY, a 469-mile scenic road which connects **GREAT SMOKY MOUNTAINS NATIONAL PARK,** located in both North Carolina and Tennessee, with Virginia's legendary Shenandoah National Park. Along the road, you'll discover panoramic overlooks, hiking trails, picnic areas, and a dozen visitors' centers, each focusing on a different aspect of this scenic land.

CHARLOTTE, North Carolina's largest city and a national hub for U.S. Airways, is a sports fan's paradise: it's home to the NBA's Hornets, the National Football League's powerful Carolina Panthers, and Charlotte Motor Speedway, a key stop on the NASCAR circuit. Paramount's CAROWINDS THEME PARK straddles the North Carolina/South Carolina border and features ten theme areas, each depicting a different segment of Carolina's past. There are thrill rides, live performances, and a whole day's worth of fun to be found here. DISCOVERY PLACE is an incredible hands-on science museum which houses such things as a planetarium, Omnimax theater, and the Science Circus.

Some 8,500 Eastern Band Cherokees have made the 56,000 acre Qualla Boundary Indian Reservation at **CHERO-KEE** their home for centuries. Be sure to visit OCANALUFTEE INDIAN VILLAGE, where Native Americans demonstrate basket making, pottery weaving, and the manufacture of canoes, arrows and blowguns.

You'll search a long time and a far distance before you find a more unusual day of fun than at **GHOST TOWN IN THE SKY** near Maggie Valley. A chairlift and an incline railway carry you 3,364 feet straight up a mountain to the main part of this Western Theme Park where you'll find saloon shows, thrill rides, gunfights, and a country music show. This is one of the liveliest days you'll ever experience.

Swiss and German settlers founded **NEW BERN,** which was the colonial capital from 1766-1776 and the state capital from 1776-1794. Its streets are lined with historic sites and outstanding examples of early 19th Century Federal style architecture. The NEW BERN CIVIL WAR MUSEUM houses one of the largest private collections of Civil War arms, uniforms and camp furniture in the country.

The **OUTER BANKS** consist of a 125-mile stretch of narrow islands and peninsulas that lie between the ocean and the sounds. CAPE HATTERAS NATIONAL SEASHORE is most extensive stretch of undeveloped seashore on the Atlantic Coast. FORT RALEIGH NATIONAL HISTORIC SITE on Roanoke Island features the ELIZABETHAN GARDENS, a re-created 16th Century formal English garden with antique statuary, period furniture and rose and herb beds. The WRIGHT BROTHERS NATIONAL MEMORIAL at Kill Devil Hills includes reproductions of the 1902 glider and the 1903 flyer.

RALEIGH has two outstanding museums: The NORTH CAROLINA MUSEUM OF ART, which features Ancient, European, American, 20th Century, Jewish ceremonial art, African, Oceanic and New World collections. The NORTH CAROLINA MUSEUM OF HISTORY, covers North Carolina history, with emphasis on folk life, sports, women's history, flight and the Civil War from pre-Colonial times to the present.

The battleship **U.S.S. NORTH CAROLINA** in Wilmington, was considered the world's greatest sea weapon when it was commissioned in 1941. It served in every major naval offensive in the Pacific in World War II. Since 1961, has served as a memorial to the 10,000 North Carolinians who died in WWII.

OLD SALEM in Winston-Salem is a living history restoration of a Moravian town of 1766-1850, with buildings, streets and gardens restored on their original sites. Costumed interpreters re-create life the way it was. For those so interested, the R.J. REYNOLDS TOBACCO/WHITAKER PARK MANUFACTURING CENTER offers guided tours of the plant, which turns out 275 million cigarettes a day. There are historical displays showing the stages of tobacco production.

Orville and Wilbur Wright made the first flight in a power-driven airplane on December 17, 1903, at Kill Devil Hills on North Carolina's wild Atlantic Coast. The day's first flight lasted 12 seconds, but by the end of the day the fragile aircraft stayed in the air a full 59 seconds—and the era of powered flight had begun.

1587

1587
REGIONAL AMERICAN CUISINE
405 Queen Elizabeth Street
Roanoke Island, North Carolina
(919) 473-1587
Dinner 5PM–10PM
AVERAGE DINNER FOR TWO: $70

T he Tranquil House Inn on the waterfront of quaint downtown Manteo on Roanoke Island is home to 1587. At this off-the-beaten-path destination, guests dine in an elegant atmosphere while gazing through large windows overlooking the Shallowbag Bay. In summer, the windows frame a spectacular moonrise.

Food is prepared with artistry and presented with flair, which has garnered the restaurant attention from national magazines and television shows.

Here, world-class chefs combine herbs from the inn's gardens with fresh Atlantic seafood, free-range and certified Angus meats and fowl and vegetables from Outer Banks growers.

The menu features such tempting dishes as Chargrilled North Atlantic Salmon over Wild Mushroom Soufflé, Louisiana Style Crawfish and Corn Chowder and Pepper-Seared Rockfish atop Asian Sautéed Vegetables.

1587'S MENU FOR FOUR

Grilled Portobello Mushroom Topped with Tarragon-Accented Vegetables

New Zealand Mussels in Mediterranean Chardonnay Broth

Jamaican Jerk Grilled Cervena Venison Fanned with Tropical Vegetable Sauté

Grilled Portobello Mushroom Topped with Tarragon-Accented Vegetables

R ub the mushrooms with the olive oil and season with salt and pepper. Grill the mushrooms until soft. Set aside.

In a medium sauté pan, heat the vegetable oil. Sauté the onions, mushroom stems, garlic and tarragon. Season with salt and pepper. If you don't have tarragon, or would like a little added flair, flambé the sautéed mixture with Sambuca liqueur. Toss in the spinach and tomatoes and finish with heavy cream and half the Asiago cheese. Cook until the cheese is melted.

To serve, top the portobello mushrooms with the vegetable mixture. Sprinkle with the rest of the Asiago cheese and broil for a minute or until the cheese on top melts.

Serves 4
Preparation Time:
   30 Minutes

   4 portobello
     mushrooms, stems cut
     off, diced and reserved
   2 Tbsps. olive oil
     Salt and pepper to
     taste
   2 Tbsps. vegetable oil
   1 small red onion,
     julienned
   2 tsps. garlic, minced
   2 Tbsps. tarragon,
     minced
     Salt and pepper to
     taste
   1 oz. Sambuca liqueur,
     optional
   1 cup packed spinach,
     roughly chopped
   2 Roma tomatoes,
     julienned
   ½ cup heavy cream
   ½ cup Asiago cheese,
     grated

New Zealand Mussels in Mediterranean Chardonnay Broth

Serves 4
Preparation Time:
  30 Minutes

- ½ yellow onion, medium dice
- ½ red pepper, medium dice
- ½ green pepper, medium dice
- 6 cremini mushrooms, sliced
- 4 Tbsps. olive oil
- 1 Tbsp. salt
- 1 Tbsp. pepper
- 4 artichoke hearts, quartered
- 2 tsps. garlic, chopped fine
- 2 sprigs sage, chopped
- 6 basil leaves, chiffonade
- 1 cup Chardonnay
- 2 cups fish stock
- 20 New Zealand mussels, shucked
- 2 Roma tomatoes, halved, sliced
- ½ cup feta cheese, crumbled

I n a 2-qt. saucepan, cook the onion, peppers and mushrooms in the olive oil, salt and pepper until moist.

Add the artichoke hearts, garlic and herbs and stir over medium heat for 2 minutes.

Add the Chardonnay and boil on high heat until reduced by half. Then add the fish stock, mussels and tomatoes and simmer for a minute or two.

Add the feta cheese and ladle into 4 soup bowls to be served immediately.

Cooking Secret: In place of fish stock, use canned clam juice.

Jamaican Jerk Grilled Cervena Venison Fanned with Tropical Vegetable Sauté

Marinate the venison in a large pan with 3 Tbsps. olive oil, raspberry or cider vinegar, 1 tsp. jerk seasoning, ½ Tbsp. garlic, salt and peppercorns. Cover with plastic wrap and refrigerate for 2 hours.

Remove the venison from the marinade and dry well with paper towels. Grill the marinated venison over hot coals, cooking evenly to desired doneness as you would any red meat.

While the venison is cooking, heat 2 Tbsps. olive oil in a medium sauté pan on high heat. Add the red onions, bell peppers, garlic and 1 tsp. jerk seasoning. When the vegetables are nearly tender, add the scallions, pineapple and tomatoes and sauté until all the ingredients are hot. Season with salt and pepper to taste.

Serves 4
Preparation Time:
  30 Minutes
(note marinating time)

  4 portions of Cervena venison leg meat, 6 oz. each
  5 Tbsps. olive oil
  2 Tbsps. raspberry vinegar or cider vinegar
  2 tsps. Jamaican jerk seasoning
1½ Tbsps. garlic, minced
  ½ tsp. kosher salt
  ½ tsp. cracked mixed peppercorns
  ½ medium red onion, medium dice
  ½ medium red bell pepper, medium dice
  ½ medium green bell pepper, medium dice
  ¼ bunch scallions, chopped into ½-inch pieces
  ½ pineapple, peeled, cored, medium dice
  2 Roma tomatoes, seeded, medium dice
    Salt and pepper to taste

★

AURORA

Aurora
NORTHERN ITALIAN CUISINE
Carr Mill Mall
Chapel Hill, North Carolina
(919) 942-2400
Lunch Monday–Friday 11:30AM–2PM
Dinner Daily 6PM–10PM
AVERAGE DINNER FOR TWO: $50

T he creative menu at Aurora is a Northern Italian feast of different courses (antipasto, primo piatto, secondo piatto, dolce) complemented by fresh-baked breads, breadsticks, wine and after-dinner espresso. Executive Chef Higgins specializes in fresh, hand-rolled pasta such as Rotelletti con Pesto Pumante—spinach pasta rolled with an herbed, three-cheese filling and baked with sun-dried tomato fresh basil sauce.

In addition to the daily specials, the menu offers such dishes as Black-Pepper Pasta Stuffed with Pumpkin and Almond Topped with a Cream Sauce, Grilled Prosciutto-Wrapped Shrimp with Caper Butter and Breast of Duck Marinated with Red Wine, Balsamic Vinegar, Citrus, Ginger and Herbs, Roasted and finished in Chianti Gelatine.

Aurora also offers an excellent selection of Italian and domestic wines.

The rustic setting of the historic Carr Mill is softened by fresh roses, pink linens and pastels, creating a contemporary dining room with a relaxed and elegant atmosphere.

AURORA'S MENU FOR FOUR

Caprino Salad

Garlic, Broccoli and White Bean Soup

Swordfish with Wild Mushroom Hash

Caprino Salad

P urée the garlic in a food processor and add the mustard powder. Slowly drizzle the balsamic vinegar, lemon juice, oils, salt and pepper into the dressing.

Toss mixed greens with the salad dressing. You will have leftover dressing. Divide the dressed greens onto 4 serving plates and top with the olives, goat cheese, walnuts, croutons and artichoke hearts.

Serves 4
Preparation Time:
  15 Minutes

  2 **garlic cloves**
 ½ **tsp. dry mustard powder**
 ¼ **cup balsamic vinegar**
  2 **Tbsps. lemon juice**
 ½ **cup olive oil**
 ½ **cup extra virgin olive oil**
 ½ **tsp. salt**
 ½ **tsp. fresh ground pepper**
  4 **cups mesclun or mixed salad greens**
 20 **Greek olives**
  4 **oz. mild goat cheese**
 ½ **cup walnuts, toasted, chopped**
 ½ **cup croutons, preferably homemade from crusty Italian bread**
  8 **marinated artichoke hearts, quartered**

☆

Garlic, Broccoli and White Bean Soup

Serves 4
Preparation Time:
  45 Minutes

    8 cups chicken stock,
      preferably homemade
    1 tsp. fresh thyme
    6 garlic cloves
    1 tsp. fresh ground
      pepper
  1½ cups white beans,
      precooked or canned
    1 cup tomatoes,
      precooked or canned,
      chopped
    1 cup broccoli, cleaned,
      coarsely chopped
    ¼ cup broccoli florets
    4 tsps. Parmesan cheese
      Parmesan croutons,
      garnish, optional

B oil the chicken stock with garlic cloves, thyme and pepper for 30 minutes. Add the beans and return to a boil. Add the tomatoes, chopped broccoli and broccoli florets. Simmer for an additional 10 minutes.

Serve each bowl of soup topped with 1 tsp. of Parmesan cheese or with a Parmesan crouton.

★

Swordfish with Wild Mushroom Hash

Dredge filets in flour and sauté in 3 Tbsps. hot olive oil until the outside is brown and crispy. Do not completely cook them, as you will put them in the oven at 300° to finish. The time of cooking will depend on the thickness of the fillets, generally a total of 10 minutes per inch of fish. Remove fish from oven and keep warm.

Heat 1 tsp. olive oil in a skillet. Add the garlic and shallots. Add the remaining vegetables and mushrooms. Sauté the vegetables for 5 minutes. Add the crab meat and stir into the vegetable mixture. Season to taste with salt and pepper. Add the lemon juice.

To serve, divide the hash into 4 portions and top each with swordfish. Top with fresh chives and lemon slices.

Serves 4
Preparation Time:
  30 Minutes
Preheat oven to 300°

4 swordfish fillets, skin removed, 6 oz. each
  Flour for dredging
3 Tbsps + 1 tsp. olive oil
1 tsp. garlic
1 tsp. shallots
2 cups Napa cabbage, core removed, sliced thin
1 zucchini, quartered, sliced into ¼-inch pieces
1 small carrot, grated
1 bunch scallions, chopped
½ lb. asparagus, sliced on a diagonal into 1-inch lengths
2 oz. shiitakes, stems removed, sliced thin
3 oz. portobello mushrooms, sliced thin
1 cup lump crab meat
  Salt and pepper to taste
1 tsp. lemon juice
  Chives, garnish
  Lemon slices, garnish

☆

THE FAIRVIEW AT THE WASHINGTON DUKE INN AND GOLF CLUB

The Fairview at the Washington Duke Inn and Golf Club
NEW AMERICAN CUISINE
3001 Cameron Boulevard
Durham, North Carolina
(919) 490-0999
Lunch and Dinner Daily 7AM–10PM
AVERAGE DINNER FOR TWO: $90

Since the late 1800s, the name Duke has been synonymous with excellence. The tradition continues at the Washington Duke Inn and Golf Club on Duke University's campus. The inn is Durham's first deluxe hotel and is home to The Fairview restaurant.

The Fairview is elegant dining at its best—furnished with antiques and Oriental rugs and provided with a commanding view of the golf course. Service here is impeccable, with your every whim anticipated—even on a busy night.

Sumptuous entrees to sample include Ginger Glazed Fillet of Salmon, Honey-Mustard and Rye-Crusted Rack of Lamb, Smoked Portobello and Cremini Mushroom Risotto, Sautéed Crab Cake and Roasted Tenderloin of Beef au Poivre. And don't miss the homemade desserts.

The wine list is well-matched to the cuisine, with the California Chardonnays and Cabernets dominating.

THE FAIRVIEW'S MENU FOR FOUR

Duck Confit with Apple and Cranberry Compote

Grilled Pork Chops with Red Pepper and Rosemary Marmalade

Creamy Yukon Gold Mashed Potatoes

Duck Confit with Apple and Cranberry Compote

Generously season the duck with the bay leaves, thyme and garlic. Place all the duck on a sheet pan and cover with a damp cloth. Place in a cooler for 24 hours. The next day, wipe away the seasoning with a damp towel. Do not rinse.

Melt the duck fat in a pot large enough so all the duck legs are submerged. Slowly heat the pot. The fat should get hot enough to cook the duck, but must never boil. Cook the duck for 2½ hours on top of the stove, uncovered. The duck is finished when the meat falls from the bone. Remove the duck from the oil and set aside.

In a heated sauté pan, melt the sweet butter. Add the apples and gently sauté until light brown and tender. Add the cranberries and sprinkle brown sugar over the mixture. Remove from heat and keep at room temperature.

To serve, remove duck meat from the bone while hot. Place a mound of the fruit compote in the center of each serving plate. Spoon the duck around and on top of the compote. Garnish with segments of fresh oranges. The citrus will go well with the richness of the duck.

Serves 4
Preparation Time:
3 Hours
(note marinating time)

4 large duck legs
2 large bay leaves, crushed
8 fresh thyme sprigs
4 garlic cloves, minced
5 cups duck fat
2 tsps. sweet butter
4 Granny Smith apples, peeled, cored, diced into 1-inch pieces
1½ lbs. dried cranberries
1 tsp. brown sugar
Orange segments, garnish

☆

Grilled Pork Chops with Red Pepper and Rosemary Marmalade

Serves 4
Preparation Time:
 1 Hour
(note marinating time)

Spice Marinade for Pork:
Yield: 1¼ cups
- 2 Tbsps. each: ground bay leaf, clove, nutmeg, paprika and thyme
- 1 Tbsp. each: ground allspice, cinnamon and savory
- 5 Tbsps. white peppercorns, ground

Pork Chops:
- 4 center cut pork chops, bone in, 12 oz. each
 Salt and pepper to taste
 Olive oil for sautéing
- 4 red peppers, julienned
- ½ cup red wine vinegar
- 1½ cups honey
- 1 cup veal demi-glace
- 5 fresh rosemary sprigs, cleaned, chopped fine

For the marinade: Blend all spices together and store in a screw-top jar. Use up to ½ tsp. per pound of meat.

For the pork chops: Trim and defat the chops. If you wish to marinate them, mix the marinade ingredients in a bowl, rub into the meat of the chops on both sides, cover and refrigerate an hour or, if possible, overnight. Dry the chops on paper towels and with season with salt and pepper after you remove them from the marinade.

In a large pot, heat the olive oil. When hot, add the red peppers and sauté them until they begin to soften. Then add the vinegar and reduce liquid by half.

Add the honey and bring back to a boil, constantly stirring. Add the demi-glace and rosemary. Taste and season with salt and pepper. The marmalade should have a sweet-and-sour rosemary flavor. Set aside.

Place pork chops on a grill at medium heat for about 8 minutes on each side or until cooked. The chops are done when the flesh feels fairly firm to the touch; it should be still juicy and faintly pink when you cut into the flesh near the bone.

To serve, spoon marmalade over each pork chop.

Creamy Yukon Gold Mashed Potatoes

Place the potatoes in a pot, completely covered with cold water and bring to boil on the stove.

When the potatoes are cooked, drain the water and mash them by hand, using a potato masher.

Add the melted butter and warmed cream. Whip potatoes by hand and season well with salt and pepper.

Serves 4
Preparation Time:
  30 Minutes

  3 lbs. Yukon gold
    potatoes, peeled,
    cubed
  ½ lb. sweet butter,
    melted
  1 cup heavy cream,
    warmed
    Salt and pepper to
    taste

★

THE MARKET PLACE

The Market Place
CONTINENTAL SOUTHERN CUISINE
20 Wall Street
Asheville, North Carolina
(704) 252-4162
Dinner Tuesday–Thursday 6PM–9PM
Dinner Friday & Saturday 6PM–9:30PM
AVERAGE DINNER FOR TWO: $60

O n a charming street in historic downtown Asheville, The Market Place presents the city's finest cuisine in an elegant setting. Widely recognized for culinary excellence, the changing menu reflects a combination of the freshest fruits, vegetables, meats and seafood, artfully prepared and served in a unique contemporary setting. Critical acclaim comes to The Market Place from a host of national publications for its originality, service and delectability.

The brushed stainless steel panels and St. Florentine rose marble that surround the dining area are outstanding examples of world-class elegance. A small courtyard flanked by painted columns and iron gating provides outdoor dining in the summertime. Large, original pastel landscapes adorn the main dining room.

Chef Tim McElrath, a native of Asheville, offers menu selections such as Cedar-Roasted Salmon with Herb Potato Crust, Sauté of Black Tiger Shrimps and Jumbo Sea Scallops in a Coconut Curry Sauce over homemade Linguine, Roasted Rack of Lamb with Goat Cheese and Wild Mushroom Garlic Flan and a Half Roast Duckling with Crispy Vegetable Spring Rolls in Sun-Dried Blueberry Port Wine Sauce.

THE MARKET PLACE'S MENU FOR SIX

Morel Mushroom Blue Cheese Gratin

Beet Soup with Sour Cream and Apple-Smoked Bacon

Grilled Mountain Trout Watercress Salad

Morel Mushroom Blue Cheese Gratin

Sauté the shallots and garlic over medium heat. Add ¼ cup of the Marsala wine and cook until dry. Add the cream and reduce by ⅓. Add the fresh thyme and blue cheese. When the cheese has melted, salt and pepper to taste.Remove from pan and set aside.

Sauté the mushrooms until tender. Deglaze the pan with ¼ cup Marsala wine. Divide the mushrooms into 6 ovenproof bowls. Add approximately 4 Tbsps. of the cream sauce to each bowl, over the mushrooms. Sprinkle all the bowls with bread crumbs and Parmesan cheese. Brown under the broiler for 2 minutes.

Serve with a crusty baguette.

Serves 6
Preparation Time:
  30 Minutes

  1 tsp. shallot
 ½ tsp. garlic
 ½ cup Marsala wine
  2 cups cream
 ½ tsp. fresh thyme
  4 oz. blue cheese
    Salt and pepper to
    taste
  1 lb. morels
    Bread crumbs, garnish
    Parmesan cheese,
    garnish

☆

Beet Soup with Sour Cream and Apple-Smoked Bacon

Serves 6
Preparation Time:
 30 Minutes

12 medium beets
 1 tsp. caraway seeds
 1 medium onion
 1 Tbsp. olive oil
 3 cups chicken stock
    Salt, pepper and
    vinegar to taste
 ½ cup sour cream,
    garnish
 ½ cup cooked, apple
    smoked bacon, cut in
    strips, garnish
 1 tsp. caraway seeds

Cook beets in salted water with caraway seeds until soft. Cool, peel and diced, reserving the liquid.

Sauté the onion in oil over medium heat until shiny, then add the diced beets. Stir for 2 minutes. Cover with stock and bring to a boil.

Remove from heat and purée in a food processor. Add the strained beet stock as needed for desired consistency. Season with salt and pepper and vinegar if desired.

Garnish with sour cream, apple-smoked bacon and caraway seeds.

Grilled Mountain Trout Watercress Salad

C lean the trout, removing as many pin bones as possible. Grill with skin on for 4 minutes on each side. Let cool and peel back skin, remove meat. Use one-half trout per salad.

Whisk together the olive oil, capers, dill, lime juice, salt and pepper in a large mixing bowl to make a vinaigrette.

Clean the watercress and lay out on a towel to dry thoroughly. Arrange the watercress and trout on plates and drizzle with vinaigrette.

Garnish with roasted red peppers for color if desired.

Serves 6
Preparation Time:
  30 Minutes

  3 **whole trout, 10 to**
    12 oz. each
¼ **cup olive oil**
  2 **tsps. capers**
  3 **tsps. fresh dill**
  3 **tsps. lime juice**
    Salt and pepper to
    taste
  1 **lb. watercress**
    Roasted red peppers,
    garnish (optional)

☆

PEWTER ROSE

Pewter Rose
INTERNATIONAL-AMERICAN CUISINE
1870 South Boulevard
Charlotte, North Carolina
(704) 332-8149
Dinner 5PM–11PM
AVERAGE DINNER FOR TWO: $50

Having been located in the historic "South-End" of Charlotte for almost 10 years, the Pewter Rose is one of the cornerstones of that newly burgeoning restaurant and entertainment district.

The Pewter Rose is housed on the second floor of a turn-of-the-century former textile-machinery warehouse, with thirty-foot, wood-beamed ceilings, twenty-foot windows and French doors. The restaurant features a charmingly eclectic mixture of furnishings—from exquisite Victorian antiques to campy '70s Naugahyde—surrounded by original local art and lush greenery. The spacious yet cozy dining room and lounge features live entertainment several nights a week and outside patio seating when weather permits.

The menu is as diverse as the atmosphere. Executive Chef Dewey offers extensive seasonal menus with diversity as his hallmark. Some of the dishes to try are Chicken-Artichoke Crepes, Whiskey Crayfish Gumbo, Kahlua Shrimp, Raspberry Salmon Salad, Chilled Peach-Riesling Soup and Black Tea-Smoked Duckling.

PEWTER ROSE'S MENU FOR SIX

Goat Cheese and Arugula Salad with Lavender-Vanilla Vinaigrette

Tenderloin with Summer Vegetables

Goat Cheese and Arugula Salad with Lavender-Vanilla Vinaigrette

For the dressing, warm the vinegar and vanilla bean in a small, non-reactive sauce pan. Allow the vanilla bean to steep for 10 minutes.

Remove pan from heat and remove the vanilla bean.

In a blender or food processor, put the cooled vinegar and all the remaining dressing, ingredients except the oil. With the blender running, slowly drizzle in the oil to emulsify.

Strain through a fine-mesh sieve. Set aside.

For the potato ribbons, peel the potato and cut into 1/8 × 1/2-inch ribbons. Soak the potato ribbons in ice water for 15 minutes or longer. Drain and pat absolutely dry.

Heat the peanut oil to 340°. Carefully scatter the potato ribbons into hot oil. Allow to cook just until they begin to brown. Remove potatoes from oil and drain on paper towels. Season to taste. Set aside.

For the salad, divide the cheese into 18 portions. Roll into balls and dip one side into pepper.

Arrange the arugula on 6 plates and put 3 balls of cheese on each plate. Drizzle dressing and scatter pumpkin seeds over the salad. Garnish with the sweet potato ribbons. Serve immediately.

Serves 6
Preparation Time:
 30 Minutes

Dressing:
 5 Tbsps. white wine
  vinegar
 1/2 vanilla bean, split
 3/4 tsp. dried lavender
  flowers
 2 Tbsps. clover honey
 1/2 tsp. ground black
  pepper
 1 tsp. Kosher salt
 3/4 cup olive oil

Potato Ribbons:
 1/2 small sweet potato
 2 cups peanut oil
 1 tsp. Kosher salt

Salad:
 12 oz. goat cheese or
  chèvre
  Fresh-ground black
  pepper to taste
 1/4 lb. arugula, heavy
  stems removed
 4 Tbsps. pumpkin seeds,
  toasted

☆

Tenderloin with Summer Vegetables

Serves 6
Preparation Time:
  1¼ Hours
(note drying time)

18 cherry tomatoes, cut
    in half
18 Roma tomatoes, cut in
    half lengthwise
    Kosher salt and fresh-
    ground black pepper
    to taste
30 asparagus stalks,
    bottom 2-inch
    removed, cut into
    3-inch pieces
 2 large red onions, sliced
    into ½-inch strips
¼ cup extra-virgin olive
    oil
12 beef tenderloin
    medallions, fully
    trimmed, 3 to 4 oz.
    each
    Madeira Broth (recipe
    follows)
 8 chive stalks, cut 1-inch
    long pieces

rrange the tomatoes on a sheet pan, cut side up and sprinkle with salt and pepper. Dry in oven at 150° for approximately 18 hours or until dry, yet pliable.

In a large sauté pan, toss the asparagus and onions in olive oil, salt and pepper. Sauté until the vegetables are done but firm. Combine the asparagus, onions and dried tomatoes in a bowl and set aside.

Parboil the potatoes in salted water; drain and dry. In a large sauté pan, brown the potatoes, cut side down, in olive oil, and season. Remove to a bowl with the vegetables and toss together.

Grill the tenderloin medallions to desired doneness. Remove the steaks from the grill and set aside.

Divide the vegetable mixture among 6 plates. Set the grilled steaks on top of the vegetables and ladle the Madeira Broth (recipe follows) over all. Garnish with fresh chives.

Cooking Secret: The vegetables and broth can be done 1 day ahead and kept.

Madeira Broth

Heat the olive oil in a large, heavy pan and sauté the celery, carrots, yellow onion, ginger, thyme, black pepper, parsley, tomato paste, garlic and bay leaves until well browned.

Deglaze the pan with Madeira and bring to a boil to cook off the alcohol. Add the rest of the ingredients. Simmer to reduce by ⅓, approximately 30 minutes.

Strain through a fine-mesh sieve, adjusting seasoning as needed.

**Preparation Time:
45 Minutes**

½ cup olive oil
⅓ cup celery, roughly chopped
⅓ cup carrots, peeled, roughly chopped
1 yellow onion, roughly chopped
⅓ cup fresh ginger, sliced
Pinch of dried thyme
Pinch of ground black pepper
3 parsley stems
1 Tbsp. tomato paste
1 large garlic clove, crushed
2 bay leaves
1¼ cups Madeira
¼ cup ginger juice
1 qt. beef stock, unsalted

☆

ARROWHEAD INN

Arrowhead Inn
106 Mason Road
Durham, North Carolina 27712
(800) 528-2207
(919) 477-8430
ROOM RATES: $95–$175

Built around 1774, the Arrowhead Inn prides itself on being "just a bit older than the United States." Spend time strolling the four acres, under 150-year-old magnolias, amid 33 varieties of birds.

While each room is decorated in a tasteful and comfortable period interpretation, the inn also believes that nostalgia leaves off where modern convenience begins. The Land Grant cabin is a honeymoon paradise with a king bed in the loft and a sitting room where you can enjoy a wood-burning fireplace. The Brittain Room also features a king bed with a wood-burning fireplace.

Asparagus And Ham Mornay

Cut bottoms off asparagus spears.
Boil water to cover the asparagus, adding salt to taste. Cook the spears for a minute, or to desired doneness. Drain.

Heat butter in a saucepan; add the flour, stirring rapidly. Add the milk, continuing to stir. Cook for 5 minutes or until thickened. Remove from heat. Stir in ¾ cup of grated cheese. Add the egg yolk, pepper, nutmeg and cayenne. Stir to blend.

Turn broiler on high. Wrap each spear of asparagus in meat. Place spears in a baking dish, slightly overlapping. Pour the sauce over the spears and sprinkle the remaining cheese on top.

Broil for 5 minutes to brown. Serve immediately.

Serves 6
Preparation Time:
  40 Minutes

24 asparagus spears
   Salt to taste
 3 Tbsps. butter
 4 Tbsps. flour
1½ cups milk
 1 cup Gruyere or Swiss
   cheese, grated
 1 egg yolk
   Pinch of freshly
   ground pepper
   Pinch of freshly grated
   nutmeg
   Pinch of cayenne
   pepper
24 prosciutto slices or
   thin-cut ham

THE GROVE PARK INN RESORT

The Grove Park Inn Resort
290 Macon Avenue
Asheville, North Carolina 28804
(800) 438-5800
(704) 252-2711
ROOM RATES: $79–$1550

When the inn opened in 1913, the Grove Park Inn Resort was hailed as "the finest resort hotel in the world." Over three-quarters of a century later, the inn has served seven American presidents, numerous dignitaries and scores of celebrities and is now recognized as one of the most important and best-preserved vestiges of the American Arts and Crafts Movement. Of course, many improvements have been made since then—including adding an indoor sports center and two new wings.

Constructed of enormous boulders—some weighing as much as 10,000 pounds—weathered stone and oak woodwork, the inn stands watch over the city of Asheville. The 510 guest rooms, including 12 suites, are located in the historic Main Inn and the Vanderbilt and Sammons wings. Deluxe and private accommodations provided on the Club Floor offer oversized guest rooms with Jacuzzis and a private Club Lounge.

Grilled Pork Chops with Green Tomato Relish

T o make the relish, combine the tomatoes, bell pepper, onion and chile together with salt in a mixing bowl. Allow to sit for 2 hours, then drain through a colander and squeeze out moisture.

In a small sauce pan, add the vinegar, sugar, mustard and celery seed and bring to a boil. Add the vegetables and simmer for an additional 2 minutes. Let cool.

Brush the pork chops with olive oil and season with salt and pepper and grill over medium heat until done, approximately 6 minutes per side.

Place chops on individual serving plates with the relish over the chops or on the side.

Cooking Secret: Make tomato relish a day ahead for optimum flavor. The relish will keep for up to two weeks.

Serves 4
Preparation Time:
 40 Minutes
(note marinating time)

 3 hard green tomatoes, finely chopped
 1 red bell pepper, finely chopped
 1 small onion, finely chopped
 1 small green chile, minced
 2 Tbsps. salt
 1 cup white vinegar
 2 Tbsps. sugar
 $\frac{1}{2}$ tsp. mustard seed
 $\frac{1}{8}$ tsp. celery seed
 4 pork chops, 8 oz. each
 1 Tbsp. olive oil
   Pepper to taste

THE HOMEPLACE BED AND BREAKFAST

The Homeplace Bed and Breakfast
5901 Sardis Road
Charlotte, North Carolina 28270
(704) 365-1936
ROOM RATES: $98–$125

S ituated on 2½ wooded acres in southeast Charlotte, the Homeplace is an oasis in one of the South's fastest growing cities. The moment you drive up to this Country Victorian bed and breakfast, your cares are left behind and a warm and friendly haven welcomes you. Built in 1902, this completely restored home has a wrap-around porch where you can pull up a rocking chair and make yourself at home. The overall feeling is one of a simpler time. While you may feel as if the rest of the world is far away, the inn is a short 15 minutes from Charlotte, where treasure hunting in the local antique shops and an assortment of fine restaurants awaits you.

The spacious bedrooms, decorated in a blend of Country and Victorian decor, feature 10-foot ceilings, heart-of-pine floors and special touches such as quilts, fine linens, handmade accessories, family antiques and original paintings.

Banana and Pineapple Cake

Mix all dry ingredients in a large bowl. Add all the remaining ingredients and mix until well blended.
Pour into a greased bundt or tube pan and bake at 350° for 1 hour or until a toothpick comes out clean.

Serves 6
Preparation Time:
  30 Minutes
Cooking Time:
  1 Hour
Preheat oven to 350°

3 cups flour
1 tsp. baking soda
1 tsp. cinnamon
2 cups sugar
1 tsp. salt
1½ cups oil
1 can crushed pineapple
  (do not drain)
1½ tsps. vanilla
3 bananas, diced,
  approximately 2 cups
3 eggs, lightly beaten

☆

PINE NEEDLES LODGE AND GOLF CLUB

Pine Needles Lodge and Golf Club
US Highway 1, N. C. Route No. 2
P.O. Box 88
Southern Pines, North Carolina 28388
(800) 747-7272
(910) 692-7111
ROOM RATES: $125-$155 Golf packages available

For three generations, legendary player and teacher Peggy Kirk Bell and her family have been welcoming guests to Pine Needles Lodge & Golf Club. Here, in one of golf's most peaceful settings, you will find the ideal vacation atmosphere in which to dramatically improve your game.

Play on a Donald Ross course, that was the site of the 1996 U.S. Women's Open, and learn techniques tailored to your ability and playing style.

While golf is the activity of choice, other amenities to enjoy are tennis, heated pools, a spa and fitness room. Dining room specialties range from Southern specialties to Continental entrees, appetizers and desserts.

Roast Duck Breast with Wild Mushroom Stuffing

R emove skin from the duck breast and trim off a thin layer of fat from the under side of skin. Remove tenderloin and process in a food process to a fine dice. Set aside for stuffing.

In a sauté pan, sweat shallots and then add mushrooms. Cook quickly over high heat, just as mushrooms begin to soften, deglaze with white wine and add fresh herbs. Cook out wine and transfer to small stainless mixing bowl and chill over ice bath.

In separate stainless bowl combine duck stuffing and cream and blend smooth. When the mushroom mix has chilled, add into the stuffing, folding carefully as to not break up mushroom pieces. Add salt and pepper to taste.

Spread a thin layer of mushroom stuffing over the duck breast. Cover with the skin tucking the skin underneath the breast on all sides (you could also truss or tie the skin around the breast for a more uniform appearance when cooked).

Place duck on roasting pan and roast at 425° for 15 minutes for a rare or longer for more well done. Take out of oven and let rest a couple of minutes Then slice on an end to end bias.

Serve duck breast on a pool of the sun-dried cherry sauce.

Cooking Secret: This recipe an silver medal winner at the IKA Culinary Olympics in Berlin in 1996.

* Forcemeat is a mixture of finely ground, raw or cooked meat, poultry, fish vegetables or fruit mixed with bread crumbs and various seasonings. The ingredients are usually ground several times to obtain a very smooth texture. A forcemeat can be used to stuff other foods or by itself.

Serves 6
Preparation Time:
  45 Minutes
Preheat oven to 425°

  6 duck breasts, boneless,
    6 to 7 oz. each
  1 Tbsp. shallots, chopped
    fine
1½ oz. chanterelle
    mushrooms, finely
    diced
  1 oz. morel mushrooms,
    finely diced
  1 oz. shiitake
    mushrooms, finely
    diced
1½ oz. cremini
    mushrooms, finely
    diced
  ¼ cup white wine
  ¼ cup forcemeat*
  2 Tbsps. cream
  2 tsps. parsley, chopped
  1 tsp. chives, sliced thin
  ½ tsp. thyme, chopped
    fine
  ½ tsp. sage, chopped fine
  ¼ tsp. rosemary, chopped
    fine
  ½ tsp. black pepper
  1 tsp. Kosher salt
    Sun-Dried Cherry
    Sauce (recipe follows)

☆

Sun-Dried Cherry Sauce

Serves 6
Preparation Time:
  15 Minutes

1½ tsps. shallots, chopped
    fine
 ½ tsp. garlic, minced
 ¼ cup Chardonnay
  9 sun-dried cherries,
    chiffonade
1½ cups duck juice
    reduction (full flavor
    and dark)
  1 tsp. arrow root mixed
    with water
    Salt and pepper to
    taste

In sauce pan cook the shallots and garlic until they just start to brown or caramelize.

Deglaze with wine. Add the sun-dried cherries and reduce. Add the duck juice and bring to boil. Add the arrow-root. Bring to a boil and remove from heat. Season to taste with salt and pepper.

Warm Roasted Corn and Black Bean Salad with Bourbon Sweet Potatoes

In a large mixing bowl, combine all the ingredients, blending well.

Allow mixture to sit at least 1 hour for flavors to marinate.

Before serving, toss quickly in a hot sauté pan to warm.

Bourbon Enhanced Sweet Potatoes

In a saucepan with water, boil the sweet potatoes until tender. Drain well and purée in a food processor.

Return sweet potatoes to a sauce pan and add the remaining ingredients. Over a low heat cook out the moisture until the potatoes have a thick consistency for piping. Adjust seasoning if needed.

Place the potatoes into a piping bag and pipe onto a serving plate. Just before serving, slightly brown under a salamander or broiler.

Serves 6
Preparation Time:
  15 Minutes
(note marinating time)

  1 cup fresh whole corn kernels, roasted
  1 cup cooked black turtle beans, cooked in chicken stock
  1/3 cup red bell pepper roasted, diced
  1/4 cup green chili, roasted, diced
  1/3 cup red onion, diced
  2 Tbsps. cilantro, chopped
  Juice from 1/2 lime
  Salt and pepper to taste

Bourbon Enhanced
  Sweet Potatoes
Serves 6
Preparation Time:
  45 Minutes

  3 large sweet potatoes, peeled, cubed
  1/4 cup bourbon
  Pinch of cinnamon
  Pinch of allspice
  2 Tbsps. honey
  Black pepper to taste

☆

RICHMOND HILL INN

Richmond Hill Inn
87 Richmond Hill Drive
Asheville, North Carolina 28806
(704) 252-7313
ROOM RATES: $135–$375

R ichmond Hill was a grand mansion built in 1889 as the private residence for Ambassador and Congressman Richmond Pearson. It was a home ahead of its time with running water, a communications system and pulley-operated elevator for transporting baggage. Following a $3 million restoration, Richmond Hill Inn reopened in 1989.

There are 12 guest rooms in the actual mansion. Decorated in a style reflecting the spirit of the 1890s, all rooms offer 20th century conveniences such as private bath, television and telephones. The third-floor rooms are named for writers who lived and worked in the Asheville area, including F. Scott Fitzgerald. These rooms have sloped ceilings and skylights plus a biography and a collection of the works of the featured author.

Each of the nine cottages features a fireplace with gas coals, pencil-post bed, spacious bathroom with separate shower and tub, porches with rocking chairs, television, telephone and ceiling fan.

Southern Biscuits

Dissolve the yeast in the warm water. Set aside until the mixture bubbles.

Stir together the dry ingredients. Cut the shortening into the dry ingredients using a pastry blender or two table knives. Stir in the buttermilk and proofed yeast. Knead lightly until a soft dough forms. Put into a buttered bowl and let rise until doubled in bulk, about 1½ hours. After the dough has risen it can be refrigerated and baked later.

When ready to bake biscuits, roll out dough on a floured board to a thickness of about 1½ inches. Cut with a 3-inch cutter and place on a greased baking pan. Let rise slightly.

Bake for about 20 minutes or until lightly browned.

Yield:
  12 biscuits
Preparation Time:
  30 Minutes
(note rising time)
Preheat oven to 400°

  1 **package dry active yeast**
  ¼ **cup warm water**
2½ **cups flour**
  ½ **tsp. baking soda**
  1 **tsp. baking powder**
  1 **tsp. salt**
  2 **Tbsps. sugar**
  ½ **cup vegetable shortening**
  1 **cup buttermilk**

Ancho Pepper and Honey-Glazed Chicken Breast with Corn and Black Bean Relish

Serves 6
Preparation Time:
 40 Minutes

Chicken:
- ¼ cup ancho peppers, chopped
- 1 cup wild honey
- ½ cup balsamic vinegar
- ¼ tsp. salt
- ¼ tsp. ground black pepper
- ¼ tsp. dill weed
- 6 chicken breasts, boneless, skinless

Corn and Black Bean Relish:
- 1 Tbsp. extra-virgin olive oil
- 1 garlic clove, minced
- 1 shallot, chopped
- 2 tomatoes, peeled, seeded, chopped
  Salt, ground black pepper and ground red pepper to taste
- 1 cup corn, cooked
- 1 cup black beans, cooked
- 2 Tbsps. cilantro, chopped

For the chicken: Preheat the grill.

Make a glaze by combining the ancho peppers, honey, balsamic vinegar, salt, black pepper and dill weed.

Coat the chicken breasts with the glaze. Grill for about 4 minutes on one side; then turn the breast over and grill an additional 4 minutes or until chicken is cooked through.

For the relish: Heat the olive oil in a medium skillet over low heat. Add the garlic and shallot, and cook slowly until translucent. Add the chopped tomatoes. Season with salt, black pepper and red pepper. Cook over medium-high heat until most of the liquid is evaporated. Chill.

When ready to serve, combine the cooked tomatoes, corn, black beans and chopped cilantro.

To serve, place a chicken breast on a plate with the Corn and Black Bean Relish to the side.

☆

Bread Pudding with Bourbon Sauce

For the bread pudding: In a large mixing bowl, lightly beat the eggs. Add the half and half, sugar and vanilla.

Toss the bread, dried fruit and chopped nuts into an 8×8×2-inch baking dish. Pour the egg mixture over and stir gently to coat all the bread.

Bake at 350° for 40 to 45 minutes or until knife inserted near center comes out clean. Set aside and keep warm.

For the bourbon sauce: In a small saucepan, combine the melted butter, sugar, beaten egg yolk and water. Cook, stirring constantly, over medium-low heat for 4 to 5 minutes, until sugar dissolves and mixture bubbles.

Remove from heat. Stir in the bourbon and serve over warm Bread Pudding.

Serves 6
Preparation Time:
 30 Minutes
Preheat oven to 350°

Bread Pudding:
 4 eggs
 2¼ cups half and half
 ¾ cup sugar
 1 Tbsp. vanilla
 4 cups stale French
  bread, cubed
 ⅓ cup dried fruit,
  chopped (golden
  raisins, dried
  cranberries, dried
  cherries or dried
  apricots)
 ⅓ cup nuts, chopped
  (pecans or walnuts)

Bourbon Sauce:
 ¼ cup butter, melted,
  cooled
 ½ cup sugar
 1 egg yolk, lightly beaten
 2 Tbsps. water
 2 Tbsps. bourbon

★

SOUTH CAROLINA: The Palmetto State

Spain tried to colonize South Carolina in 1526 and failed. France tried to colonize it in 1562 and failed. The English finally succeeded, founding Charles Towne in 1670. The cultivation of indigo, rice and cotton and trade with the local Indian population brought prosperity to the new colony. Imaginative advertising soon lured hordes of English, Scottish, Spanish and French pioneers. One such poster hearkened the land, "in the same latitude as Palestine" as "beautiful with odoriferous plants, green all year…the orange and the lemon thrive in the same common orchard with the apple and the pear tree, plums, peaches, apricots and nectarines."

South Carolinians were the first to object to the Stamp Act of 1765, and they played an important part in the Revolution. It was the 8th state admitted to the Union. But independent-minded South Carolina, made prosperous by King Cotton and cheap slave labor, was also the first state to agitate for more independence from the federal government. Senator John C. Calhoun successfully argued for states' rights and South Carolina nullified the federal Tariff Act of 1832. South Carolina was also the first state to secede from the Union on December 20, 1860, and the Civil War formally began when Confederate forces fired on and captured Fort Sumter in Charleston harbor.

The Civil War and Reconstruction were devastating for South Carolina. One-fourth of its army was killed. Then carpetbaggers—economic opportunists from the North—raided the treasury and bankrupted the state. Faced with the destruction of its agricultural economy, South Carolinians turned to the textile industry. World War I gave a temporary boost to agriculture, but the boll weevil and the Great Depression wiped out much of the regrowth.

The 1950s and 60s were turbulent. The civil rights movement and forced integration raised tensions in the state, but eventually South Carolina, whose motto is, "While I breathe, I hope," accepted the inevitable with the charm and vitality that have marked the state since its beginnings. Hurricane Hugo, one of the most destructive storms in history, caused more than $7 billion worth of damage, but the folk from "South Calinky" once again rose to rebuild from adversity.

Today, South Carolina continues to rely on the manufacturing of natural and synthetic textile fibers, but tourism—particularly along the Grand Strand and in the fabled city of

Charleston—has continued to grow. The state's popularity as a retirement community has added fuel to an already vibrant economy, and its newest industries, the manufacture of motors and automobile parts, have ensured its economic health. Tobacco and sugar cane are the primary crops today, although South Carolina is no longer a primarily agricultural state.

Famous South Carolinians include John C. Calhoun, Andrew Jackson, Jesse Jackson and Strom Thurmond.

Here are some of the highlights of a trip to South Carolina.

Preservation is the order of the day in **CHARLESTON,** so much so that this city of 73 pre-Revolutionary buildings, 136 buildings from the late 1700s, 600 from the early 1800s, and more than 2,000 historic buildings altogether, is truly the last bastion of slower-paced Southern gentility. The story is told of a wealthy matron who was often asked why she didn't spend money on travel. "But my dear," she answered, "why should I travel when I'm already here?" Charleston is filled with both double houses—a standard house with front door and two flanking rooms—and single houses, where the house is literally turned on its side, with the side facing the street being only one room wide. This is because landowners were taxed based on the width of their homes' street exposure!

Park your car and walk if you really want to see the historic section, for you'll find negotiating the narrow, busy streets to be both slow and difficult. Traverse THE BATTERY, home of the city's earliest fortifications. Among the "must see" buildings, many of which contain Charleston's legendary gardens, are BETH ELOHIM, the Greek Revival design synagogue built in 1840. Originally organized in 1740, it is the oldest synagogue in continuous use in the nation, and was the first to introduce the Reform service in 1824.

CALHOUN MANSION, a Victorian built in 1876, was one of the most elaborate showplaces in the Old South. The DOCK STREET THEATER opened in 1736 as America's first building designed solely for theatrical performances. The EDMONSTON-ALSTON HOUSE (1828), the JOSEPH MANIGAULT HOUSE (1803), the NATHANIEL RUSSELL HOUSE (1808) and the HEYWARD-WASHINGTON HOUSE (1772), where George Washington actually did stay when he visited Charleston in 1791, are particularly elegant and noteworthy examples of period architecture, fully furnished now as they were when they were built. The HUGUENOT CHURCH (Gothic architecture) and ST.

★

MICHAEL'S EPISCOPAL CHURCH (1751) are two noteworthy houses of worship in a city where so many were built that Charleston was once nicknamed "The Holy City."

Charleston is surrounded by the elegance of plantations. MIDDLETON PLACE, 14 miles northwest of the city, features the oldest landscaped gardens in America (1741). It took 100 slaves 10 years to complete its terraces, camellia-lined walks and ornamental lakes. MAGNOLIA PLANTATION AND GARDENS, 10 miles northwest of Charleston, was acquired in 1676 by the Drayton family, whose heirs still own it and walk among the 900 varieties of camellias, 250 types of azaleas and hundreds of other plants that provide year-round color on some 500 acres. Here you'll also find a 16th century horticultural maze, an ante-bellum cabin and a pre-Revolutionary Greek Revival plantation house. DRAYTON HALL, built in 1738, is an outstanding example of Georgian Palladian architecture, which is virtually in its original condition: no electricity, no modern plumbing, no central heating.

To visit Charleston and not take a boat trip to **FORT SUMTER NATIONAL MONUMENT,** built on a man-made island in the middle of Charleston Harbor, is to miss a significant and meaningful part of Southern history. The brick fortification here was constructed between 1829 and 1860. On April 12, 1861, after two days of bombardment, Confederate troops captured the small garrison on the island, thus precipitating the Civil War. They continued to occupy the fort until February 1865, frustrating the Union's attempt to blockade the critical port of Charleston. Today the brick fort contains impressive breastworks, large cannon and projectiles fired both from and at the fort during the Civil War. FORT MOULTRIE, across the channel from Fort Sumter and also part of the National Monument, played an important role in the Revolutionary War.

The **GRAND STRAND,** sixty miles of inland towns and wide beachfront, culminate at **MYRTLE BEACH,** the largest and most popular vacation community in the area. One of the South's primary golf and tennis resorts, so many new Country and Western establishments have proliferated that it's also known as "Branson East." BROADWAY AT THE BEACH, a 350-acre entertainment complex, houses theaters, nightclubs, restaurants and shops. The DIXIE STAMPEDE provides a four-course meal, a performance in the Dixie Belle Saloon and a

North vs. South arena rivalry that includes feats of horsemanship, special effects and audience participation. Much the same is to be found at MEDIEVAL TIMES DINNER AND TOURNAMENT, where you'll use your hands to eat a lusty meal in a European-style castle while watching an 11th century royal tournament of jousting, dressage maneuvers, hand-to-hand combat and thrilling horsemanship. FANTASY HARBOUR gives you the RONNIE MILSAP THEATER, the GATLIN BROTHERS THEATER, the CAROLINA OPRY and, if you ever get tired of Country and Western entertainment, SNOOPY'S MAGIC ON ICE, which combines illusions, cabaret dancing and professional ice skating.

HILTON HEAD ISLAND, the largest island between New Jersey and Florida, is also one of the last unpolluted marine estuaries on the East Coast. You can see ruins of historic plantations. The freed slave "Gullah" population took over the island after the Civil War. Today, with the addition of 300 tennis courts, 25 golf courses, riding stables, bicycle trails and marinas, the island has become a magnet for vacationers. The MCI Heritage Golf Classic is held each April and the Hilton Head Island Celebrity Golf Tournament is at played at the Palmetto Dunes and Shipyard golf courses in September.

Tobacco field with wagon and sled, c. 1900

82 QUEEN

82 Queen
LOW COUNTRY CUISINE
82 Queen Street
Charleston, South Carolina
(803) 723-7591
Lunch Daily 11:30AM–2:30PM
Dinner Daily 5:30PM–10PM
AVERAGE DINNER FOR TWO: $65

Specializing in "Low Country" cuisine, 82 Queen was voted the best overall restaurant in Charleston by locals. "Low Country" refers to the geographical area between Savannah, Ga., and Pawley's Island, S.C.

Housed in a refurbished carriage house and two restored 18th-century townhouses, 82 Queen excels in casual elegance. There are seven dining rooms, adjoined by an open-air courtyard designed around wrought-iron arches purchased from Margaret Mitchell's estate.

Co-owner/chef Steve Kish was named "Cook of the Year" and lives up to the honor. Mouth-watering specialties include a Grilled Rosemary Marinated Lamb Loin with a Roasted Garlic Cabernet Sauce; an Oven-Roasted Veal Chop Stuffed with Wild Rice, Portobello Mushrooms and Sundried Tomatoes; and a Mixed Grill of Filet Mignon, Georgia Lamb and Carolina Quail. And don't miss "Low Country" favorites—Barbecued Shrimp Served over Grits and for dessert, Bourbon Pecan Pie. The restaurant boasts an extensive wine list.

82 QUEEN'S MENU FOR SIX

McCellenville Crabcakes

Charleston She-Crab Soup

Pumpkin Marble Cheesecake

McCellenville Crabcakes

In a large mixing bowl, combine the crab meat, mayonnaise, onions, Tabasco, Worcestershire sauce, ½ cup bread crumbs, lemon juice and thyme, mixing together thoroughly.

Form into cakes, about 4 oz. each.

Make an egg wash by beating together the eggs and half and half.

Dip the crab cakes in the egg mixture, then roll in the remaining bread crumbs.

Sauté in butter or olive oil until golden brown.

Serves 6
Preparation Time:
  10 Minutes

  1 **lb. lump crab meat**
  ½ **cup mayonnaise**
  2 **green onions, finely**
     chopped
  2 **dashes Tabasco**
     Dash of Worcestershire
     sauce
  ¾ **cup coarse bread**
     crumbs
  1 **Tbsp. fresh lemon juice**
  ½ **tsp. thyme, ground**
  2 **eggs**
  ¼ **cup half and half**
     Butter or olive oil

★

Charleston She-Crab Soup

Serves 8 to 10
Preparation Time:
 35 Minutes

¼ lb. butter
¼ lb. flour
 3 cups milk
 1 cup heavy cream
 2 cups fish stock or
   water with fish base
¼ lb. crab roe
 1 lb. white crab meat
 1 cup celery, chopped,
   sautéed
¼ cup carrots, chopped
¼ cup onions, chopped
 1 Tbsp. Tabasco
 1 Tbsp. Worcestershire
¼ cup sherry, garnish

I n a large sauce pot, melt the butter, then add the flour. Add the milk and cream and bring the mixture to a boil. Add the remaining ingredients (except sherry) and simmer for 20 minutes. Garnish with sherry.

Cooking Secret: This award-winning recipe was chosen by the citizens of Charleston in 1994 as the best She-Crab Soup in the city.

Pumpkin Marble Cheesecake

Combine the ginger snap crumbs, pecans and margarine and press into the bottom of a 9-inch springform pan. Bake at 325° for 10 minutes.

Combine the cream cheese, ½ cup sugar and vanilla and mix well. Add eggs and mix until fluffy. Set aside.

In another bowl, mix the reserved softened cream cheese, remaining sugar, pumpkin and spices.

Pouring into the pie crust, alternate the cream cheese filling and pumpkin mixture. After both mixtures are poured, cut through the mixture with a knife for marbled effect.

Bake in 350° oven for 55 minutes or until toothpick inserted in center comes out clean. Cool for several hours before removing from pan.

Serves 6
Preparation Time:
  1¼ Hours
Preheat oven to 325°

1½ cups ginger snap
    crumbs
 ½ cup pecans, chopped
 ¼ cup margarine, melted
 1 lb. cream cheese,
    slightly softened
    (reserve 1 cup)
 ¾ cup sugar
 1 tsp. vanilla
 3 eggs
 1 cup canned pumpkin
 ¼ tsp. ground nutmeg
 1 tsp. cinnamon

☆

COLLECTOR'S CAFÉ

Collector's Café
MEDITERRANEAN CUISINE
7726 North Kings Highway
Myrtle Beach, South Carolina
(803) 449-9370
Lunch and Dinner Monday–Saturday Noon to Midnight
AVERAGE DINNER FOR TWO: $70

T he palette and the palate get equal attention at Collector's Café, a fine dining place that's also one of the largest contemporary fine arts galleries in the Southeast. There are four separate eating areas, each with its own individual personality. The prime dining area is called "The Main Gallery." The walls are painted with the colors of the rain forest and old Greek-style columns separate large oil paintings. A more casual area is the "Grill Room," featuring tiled tables with bar chairs and a hand-painted tile bar surrounding the cooking area. The "Gallery" is a dramatically lighted dining area with watercolors, acrylics and mosaic tile art hanging from the blue and silver sponged walls.

While the menu changes seasonally, dishes worth sampling include Grilled Thai Shrimp with Cucumber Salsa and Hot Pepper Peanut Sauce, Zucchini and Carrot Pancake with Sautéed Garlic Shrimp and Mixed Grill of Pesto-Rubbed Chicken Breast, Shrimp and Beef Fillet Medallions.

COLLECTOR'S CAFÉ'S MENU FOR FOUR

Duck Confit with Hummus, Spiced Tomato and Phyllo

Wild Mushroom Soup with Lobster and White Port

Grilled Salmon Fillet with Persian Tabbouleh and Honey Balsamic Vinaigrette

Duck Confit with Hummus, Spiced Tomato and Phyllo

I n a medium-sized, ovenproof pot, place the duck, bay leaf, thyme, peppercorns and salt with enough duck fat or oil to cover up to ½-inch mark on all the ingredients. Bring to a simmer on top of the stove. Cover and place in a 350° oven for 2½ hours. Remove and cool. Pick duck meat off, discarding bones and skin. Reserve at room temperature.

For the hummus, combine the chickpeas, tahini paste, lemon juice, garlic and water in a blender and purée. Set aside.

For the assembly, place 1 heaping Tbsp. of hummus into the middle of each serving plate. Top with 1 level Tbsp. of the duck confit, 2 Tbsps. spiced tomato sauce (recipe follows), ½ tsp. rosemary oil and 1 phyllo triangle (recipe follows).

Top each serving with mizuma and frisée. Drizzle the tomato sauce and rosemary oil around the plate and garnish with rosemary sprigs.

Serves 4
Preparation Time:
 3 Hours
Preheat oven to 350°

 1 **leg and 1 thigh from a**
   4-lb. duck
 1 **bay leaf**
 4 **fresh thyme sprigs**
 ½ **tsp. cracked black**
   peppercorns
 ½ **tsp. salt**
   Rendered duck fat or
   oil
 1¼ **cups chickpeas,**
   cooked
 ¼ **cup tahini paste**
   Juice of 1 lemon
 2 **Tbsps. roasted garlic**
 3 **Tbsps. water**
   Spiced Tomato Sauce
   (recipe follows)
   Rosemary oil
   Phyllo Triangles
   (recipe follows)
 ¼ **cup mizuma leaves**
 ¼ **cup frisée**
   Fresh rosemary,
   garnish

★

Spiced Tomato Sauce and Phyllo Triangles

Preparation Time:
 40 Minutes
Preheat oven to 350°

1½ lbs. tomatoes, seeded,
    peeled, chopped
 ½ cup sugar
 ¼ tsp. allspice
 ½ tsp. cinnamon
 ¼ tsp. cloves
 ½ cup orange juice
 ¼ cup cornstarch
    dissolved in ½ cup
    water
 3 phyllo sheets
    Extra virgin olive oil

For the spiced tomatoes, simmer the tomatoes, sugar, allspice, cinnamon, cloves and orange juice in a medium-sized pot for 15 minutes. Add the cornstarch to thicken. Cool and reserve at room temperature.

For the phyllo, lay one phyllo sheet on a work surface. Brush with olive oil. Lay the second phyllo sheet over the first sheet and brush with oil. Repeat the process for the third sheet.

Cut the sheets into 2-inch triangles.

Bake at 350° until browned, according to manufacturer's directions.

Wild Mushroom Soup with Lobster and White Port

Sauté the mushrooms, carrot, celery and leek over medium heat until the liquid evaporates and the vegetables are lightly browned.

Deglaze the pan with wine and port. Reduce by ¼.

Add the cream and broth. Reduce the heat and simmer for 30 minutes. Purée the soup in a blender.

To serve, pour the soup into wide, shallow bowls. Place 1 oz. of lobster meat in the center of each bowl of soup and garnish with tarragon leaves on top.

Serves 4
Preparation Time:
  45 Minutes

  1 lb. mushrooms, sliced
  ¼ lb. shiitakes, stemmed, sliced
  ¼ lb. portobello mushrooms, grilled, sliced
  1 small carrot, chopped
  1 celery rib, chopped
  1 small leek, chopped
  ½ cup dry white wine
  ¼ cup white port
  1 cup heavy cream
  2 cups chicken broth
  ¼ lb. lobster meat, cooked, diced, garnish
     Fresh tarragon leaves, garnish

★

Grilled Salmon Fillet with Honey Balsamic Vinaigrette

Serves 4
Preparation Time:
  30 Minutes

  2 **Tbsps. balsamic**
     vinegar
 ¼ **cup honey**
  1 **cup extra-virgin olive**
     oil
     Pinch of salt
  1 **cup cilantro leaves**
  4 **salmon fillets, skinless,**
     boneless
  1 **tsp. each: ground**
     cardamom and
     coriander
  1 **red bell pepper, diced,**
     roasted
  1 **yellow bell pepper,**
     diced, roasted
     Cilantro sprigs, garnish

repare the vinaigrette in a blender by puréeing together the balsamic vinegar, honey, ½ cup extra-virgin olive oil and salt. Set aside.

For the cilantro oil, blanch the cilantro for 10 seconds. Purée with ½ cup extra-virgin olive oil and salt. Set aside.

Lightly dust the salmon fillets with spices. Grill to medium rare.

To serve, mound 1 cup tabbouleh (recipe follows) in the center of each serving plate. Top with a salmon fillet and drizzle the cilantro oil and honey vinaigrette around the tabbouleh and on top at the salmon. Sprinkle pepper around the tabbouleh. Top salmon with roasted peppers and cilantro sprigs.

Persian Tabbouleh

In a large sauté pan, wilt the onion and garlic in extra-virgin olive oil over medium heat.

Add the spices, bay leaf, saffron, fruits and nuts. Cook over medium heat for 2 minutes. Deglaze the pan with broth.

Pour the mixture over the tabbouleh in a separate bowl. Stir, then cover and let sit for 30 minutes before serving.

Serves 4
Preparation Time:
  45 Minutes

¼ cup onion
2 garlic cloves, minced
1 Tbsp. extra-virgin olive oil
1 tsp. cumin
1 tsp. cardamom
1 tsp. powdered ginger
1 tsp. cinnamon
1 bay leaf
  Pinch of saffron threads
¼ cup dried currants
¼ cup dried apricots, diced
¼ cup almonds
¼ cup cashews
¼ cup pine nuts
1¼ cups chicken broth
1¼ cups tabbouleh

MAGNOLIAS UPTOWN/DOWN SOUTH

Magnolias Uptown/Down South
NEW SOUTHERN CUISINE
185 East Bay Street
Charleston, South Carolina
(803) 577-7771
Lunch and Dinner 11:30AM–11PM
AVERAGE DINNER FOR TWO: $65

Decorated in black and white, with soft track-lighting and oversized paintings of magnolias on the walls, Magnolias Uptown/Down South exudes elegance and style. Three dining rooms boast columns rising from shiny, slate-tile floors, and rails decorated with iron magnolia leaves and blossoms. The Veranda Bar, highlighted by a stunning curved bar of antique heart of pine and black granite, separates the dining areas.

The most elegant dining room is "The Galley," with a more intimate ambiance created by black walls and carpeting, white, fluted wooden columns and formal draperies. Candles in iron magnolia leaf holders brighten each table and the walls have additional pieces of the "Magnolia Suite" monotype series, including the striking oil portrait of "Mama Magnolia."

Chef Donald Barickman's and Magnolias' signature entree is Spicy Shrimp, Sausage and Tasso Gravy over Creamy White Grits. Other menu highlights include Down South Egg Roll, Grilled Portobello Mushroom Cap, Carolina Carpetbagger Filet, and Sweet Potato Pie with White Chocolate and Bourbon Sauce.

MAGNOLIAS UPTOWN/DOWN SOUTH'S MENU FOR FOUR

Spicy Shrimp, Sausage and Tasso Gravy over Creamy White Grits

Pan-Fried Chicken Livers with Caramelized Onions, Country Ham and Red-Eye Gravy

Spicy Shrimp, Sausage and Tasso Gravy over Creamy White Grits

Bring 12 cups chicken broth to a boil in a heavy-bottomed stock pot or large saucepan. Slowly pour in the grits, stirring constantly. Reduce the heat to low and continue to stir so the grits do not settle to the bottom and scorch. In about 5 minutes, the grits will plump up and become a thick mass.

Continue to cook the grits for about 20 to 25 minutes, stirring frequently. The grits should have absorbed all the chicken stock and become soft. Stir in heavy cream and cook for another 10 minutes, stirring frequently. The grits should have a thick consistency and be creamy, like oatmeal. Season to taste. Keep warm over low heat until ready to serve.

For the gravy, melt the butter in a heavy-bottomed saucepan over low heat. Add the Tasso ham. Sauté for 1 minute, browning slightly. Make a roux by adding the flour and stirring until well combined.

Continue to cook over low heat for 5 minutes, stirring frequently until the roux develops a nutty aroma. Turn the heat up to medium and gradually add 2 cups of chicken broth, stirring vigorously. Keep stirring constantly until the broth begins to thicken and is smooth. Gradually add another 2 cups of broth, stirring constantly until the broth thickens into gravy. Add the parsley. Simmer for another 5 minutes. Season to taste.

Place the Italian sausage on a baking sheet with raised sides. Place on the top rack of a 400° oven and bake for 10 to 15 minutes, or until the sausage is firm and its juices run clear. Cool and cut into small, bite-sized pieces.

Heat the olive oil in a heavy-bottomed frying pan over medium heat. Add the precooked sausage and sauté for 2 minutes to brown slightly. Add the shrimp and sauté until they begin to turn pink—no longer than a minute. Add 1 cup of the chicken broth to deglaze the pan. Add the Tasso Gravy and 1 Tbsp. of the parsley. Bring to a boil and let simmer for 1 minute. The last ½ cup of the chicken stock is to be used to thin the gravy if needed.

Divide the hot grits between 8 warm bowls. Spoon the shrimp-sausage mixture over the grits. Sprinkle with the remaining parsley and serve immediately.

Serves 8
Preparation Time:
  45 Minutes
Preheat oven to 400°

17½ cups chicken broth
 4½ cups coarse, stone-ground white grits
  1 cup heavy cream
    Salt and white pepper to taste
  4 Tbsps. butter
 ½ cup sliced Tasso ham, cut in 1-inch strips
 ½ cup flour
  2 Tbsps. parsley, finely chopped
 ¾ lb. spicy Italian sausage
  2 Tbsps. olive oil
  2 lbs. medium or large shrimp, peeled, deveined
  2 Tbsps. parsley, finely chopped

★

Pan-Fried Chicken Livers with Caramelized Onions, Country Ham and Red-Eye Gravy

Serves 4
Preparation Time:
 45 Minutes
Preheat oven to 350°

  3 Tbsps. olive oil
  2 cups yellow onion, cut into ¼-inch slices, about 1 large onion
  2 cups chicken livers (about 1 lb.)
½ cup flour
  1 tsp. salt
  1 tsp. black pepper
⅓ lb. country ham, very thinly sliced
  Madeira Sauce (recipe follows)
  Red-Eye Gravy (recipe follows)

Heat 1 tsp. of olive oil in a heavy-bottomed frying pan over high heat until the oil is smoking. Lay the onion slices in the hot oil. You want to keep the slices intact and not loosen them into rings until after the initial searing. Leave them there for 1 or 2 minutes without turning, to start the caramelization process. Cook, tossing occasionally, until the onions caramelize and turn golden brown. At this point the slices may break out into rings. Watch the heat and reduce it slightly if it appears that the onions are beginning to burn. Another teaspoon of oil may be added if the pan becomes dry and the bottom begins to scorch. The caramelization process should take 6 to 10 minutes. When the onions have browned, remove them from the heat until ready to serve.

Trim any fat from the chicken livers. Rinse under cold water, then leave them in a bowl of cold water for 5 minutes to remove any residual blood. Remove the livers from the water and place them on absorbent paper towels to drain, as any excess water will splatter when the chicken livers are placed in the hot oil.

Combine the flour, salt and black pepper, mixing well. Dust the chicken livers with the seasoned flour, making certain to cover them completely so there are no wet spots showing. Shake off any excess flour so it does not burn in the pan.

Heat the remaining olive oil in a heavy-bottomed frying pan over medium-high heat. Gently place the livers in the hot oil and cover with a lid or splatter guard. Sauté them on one side for 1 to 2 minutes until golden. Uncover the pan, flip the livers over and shake the pan. If all the oil has been absorbed, add a little more, a teaspoon at a time.

Place the livers in a 350° oven for 3 to 4 minutes, or until they are firm and their centers are cooked through. While the livers are cooking, sauté the ham in a heavy-bottomed frying pan over medium heat until the edges curl up. Add the caramelized onions to the frying pan to reheat while the livers are cooking.

✮

When ready to serve, remove the livers from the oven. Put them on a plate and place the ham around them. Mound the onions in the center. Spoon Madeira Sauce (recipe follows) and Red-Eye Gravy (recipe follows) around the ham, livers and onions. Serve immediately.

Cooking Secret: The caramelized onions could be cooked ahead. However, the livers and ham are best when cooked right before serving.

Madeira Sauce

Yield:
  About 1½ cups
Preparation Time:
  25 Minutes

1½ qts. veal stock
1 Tbsp. olive oil
1 cup yellow onion,
    chopped
1 Tbsp. garlic, chopped
2 cups tomatoes,
    chopped, with juice
    and seeds
¼ cup parsley stems,
    chopped
1 cup red wine
1 cup Madeira wine
  Salt and white pepper
    to taste

In a large saucepan reduce the veal stock by half over medium heat.

Heat the olive oil in a heavy-bottomed saucepan. Add the onions, garlic, tomatoes and parsley stems and sauté for 1 minute. Add the red wine and Madeira and bring the mixture to a boil. Lower the heat and simmer gently until the liquid is reduced by two-thirds.

Add the reduced veal stock to the rest of the ingredients, and continue to reduce by simmering. You will get a nice, dark color and intensified flavor as the liquid reduces. Reduce the liquid by one-third, to approximately 2½ cups. Strain the mixture, pressing all the juices out of the vegetables, then strain again through a fine sieve.

Return the sauce to the stove and reduce the volume by another third, skimming off any foam that may come to the top. At this point you may strain once more through cheesecloth or a very fine sieve, or you may serve the sauce as it is.

Season with salt and white pepper to taste and a splash more Madeira, if desired.

Cooking Secret: It is important not to add any salt during the cooking process, because it would concentrate as the liquids are reduced.

☆

Red-Eye Gravy

H eat the olive oil in a heavy-bottomed pan over medium heat. Add the ham and sauté, stirring, for 2 minutes or until the bottom of the pan begins to turn golden and the ham browns. Add the onion and garlic and sauté, stirring for another 2 minutes. Add the coffee. Deglaze the pan, scraping up all the bits of ham, onion and garlic, as well as the browned juices. Let the coffee cook dry, then add the butter. Make the roux by adding the flour to the melted butter and stirring until well combined. Continue to cook over low heat for 5 minutes, stirring very frequently, until the roux develops a light golden color and has a nutty aroma.

Turn the heat up to medium and gradually add 1 cup of the chicken broth, stirring vigorously. Keep stirring constantly until the broth begins to thicken and its smooth. Add the remaining cup of broth, stirring constantly until the broth thickens into a gravy. Continue to simmer over low heat for 15 minutes to cook out the starchy flavor.

Serve immediately or keep warm without cooking further until ready. Season to taste. The country ham will probably make adding salt unnecessary.

Yield:
  2 cups
Preparation Time:
  30 Minutes

  1 tsp. olive oil
  ¼ cup country ham,
    chopped
  2 Tbsps. yellow onion,
    finely minced
  ½ tsp. garlic, minced
  ½ cup strong black coffee
  2 Tbsps. unsalted butter
  ¼ cup flour
  2 cups chicken broth
    Salt and freshly
    ground black pepper
    to taste

1790 HOUSE BED AND BREAKFAST

1790 House Bed and Breakfast
630 Highmarket Street
Georgetown, South Carolina 29440
(800) 890-7432
(803) 546-4821
ROOM RATES: $75–$125

When Georgetown's rice plantation culture was at its peak, this home was the center of social activity. Today, innkeepers Patricia and John Wiley beckon guests to step back to that time. The historic bed and breakfast offers six lovely guest rooms with private baths and features early Colonial and Victorian furnishings.

There's also a large drawing room with a fireplace, a beautiful dining room, a parlor-game room and a large wraparound veranda facing other historic homes, as well as the inn's scenic gardens.

Guests may enjoy breakfast on the veranda or in the dining room. Afterward you may want to stroll or bike or ride the seaport tram through the historic district. Visit shops and restaurants or the Harborwalk or venture to beaches at Pawley's Island or Huntington Beach State Park.

Back at the inn, guests are invited to enjoy late afternoon refreshments, a selection of board games, reading or a game of table tennis.

Southern Frittata

I n a medium bowl, beat the eggs, add the milk, onion, butter and seasonings. Whisk until well blended. Add the potatoes and mushrooms.

Spray Pam or oil a 9×9-inch or 2-quart baking dish. Pour the egg mixture into baking dish. Sprinkle the cheese over the egg mixture and top with bacon pieces.

Bake at 400° for 30 to 40 minutes, or until golden brown and the middle has risen.

Serves 6 to 8
Preparation Time:
  40 Minutes
Preheat oven to 400°

  6 eggs
  1 cup milk
  2 to 3 green onions or
    ¼ onion, chopped
  2 Tbsps. butter, melted
  ½ tsp. dry mustard
  ½ tsp. white pepper
  ¼ tsp. garlic powder
  ½ cup frozen or cooked
    potatoes, diced
  3 mushrooms, chopped
  1 cup cheddar cheese,
    shredded
  ½ lb. bacon, cooked
    crispy, crumbled

JOHN RUTLEDGE HOUSE INN

John Rutledge House Inn
116 Broad Street
Charleston, South Carolina 29401
(800) 476-9741
(803) 723-7999
ROOM RATES: $125–$295

Built in 1763 by John Rutledge, one of the signers of the Constitution of the United States, the inn was visited by George Washington. Designated a National Historic Landmark, the John Rutledge House Inn has been restored with beautiful details of the home's 18th and 19th century architecture: the elaborate carved Italian marble fireplace, the original plastic moldings, the inlaid floorwork and the elegant ironwork.

She-Crab Soup, a Charleston delicacy, was created here during a formal dinner in the 1920s by the butler, who was asked to dress up the plain soup generally served. The butler added the orange-hued crab eggs, which enhanced the color and flavor. This was the beginning of a tradition synonymous with Charleston cuisine.

The inn offers 19 guest rooms within a complex of three buildings. Antiques and period reproductions give each room its individual personality.

Carrot, Zucchini and Apple Muffins

Mix all of the ingredients except the eggs and oil in a large bowl.

In a separate bowl, beat the eggs and oil together. Stir into the flour mixture. Spoon ¼ cup batter into each muffin tin.

Bake at 375° for 25 minutes. Serve warm or at room temperature.

Yield:
  24 muffins
Preparation Time:
  25 Minutes
Preheat oven to 375°

  2 cups all-purpose flour
  2 cups carrots, grated
  1 cup sugar
  1 cup zucchini, grated
  1 golden apple, cored, finely chopped
  ¾ cup golden raisins
  ¾ cup coconut
  ½ cup almonds, coarsely chopped
  1 tsp. cinnamon
  2 tsps. orange peel, grated
  1 tsp. vanilla
  ½ tsp. salt
  3 large eggs
  1 cup vegetable oil

LITCHFIELD BEACH AND GOLF RESORT

Litchfield Beach and Golf Resort
Highway 17 South
Pawley's Island, South Carolina 29585
(800) 845-1897
(803) 237-3000
ROOM RATES: $49–$375

A historic plantation setting in South Carolina's scenic Low Country is home to lush, green fairways and a luxurious getaway. Located only 20 minutes south of Myrtle Beach, Litchfield Beach and Golf Resort has long been a favorite retreat for families. Nestled on 4,500 acres of garden-like grounds, the resort whisks guests away from the world and all its hassles.

That's why Litchfield often finds its way onto lists of top resorts in the country. The resort is a combination of oceanfront condominiums, scenic lake view villas, fairway cottages and spacious hotel suites. Suites are tastefully decorated in pastels and light woods and feature marble baths, wet bars, refrigerators and microwave ovens.

Guests may enjoy the resort's three signature 18-hole golf courses, 19 tennis courts, racquetball courts, health and beauty spa, on-site dining and miles of beautiful beach.

Popover Ragout of Quail

For the popovers, blend together the eggs, milk, flour, salad oil, nutmeg and salt. Fill 6 well-greased muffin tins ¾ full.

Bake at 375° for 20 minutes. Remove from oven to cool.

In a large sauté pan, heat the hazelnut oil. Dredge quail breasts and legs in flour. Put in the pan and sauté until brown. Leaving the quail pieces in the pan, deglaze with Madeira. Add the mushrooms and chicken stock and reduce the liquid by ⅓.

Cut off the tops of the popovers and set aside.

On 6 plates, portion out the ragout, using 1 breast and 2 legs each, arranging the stew in and around the popover. Replace the tops and garnish each with a sprig of rosemary.

Serves 6
Preparation Time:
  30 Minutes
Preheat oven to 375°

  4 eggs
  1 cup milk
1½ cups flour
  ¼ cup salad oil
  ½ tsp. nutmeg
    Pinch of salt
  ⅓ cup hazelnut oil
  6 quail breasts, skinless
12 quail legs
  1 cup flour
  ¾ cup Madeira
  1 lb. dried mushrooms, rinsed, drained
  3 cups chicken stock
  6 rosemary sprigs

☆

THE RHETT HOUSE INN

The Rhett House Inn
1009 Craven Street
Beaufort, South Carolina 29902
(803) 524-9030
ROOM RATES: $125–$195

Nestled in historic Beaufort, South Carolina, is an authentic inn that beautifully recreates the feeling of the "old" South, when this was the most cultivated and enchanting town of its size in America.

The living room, where guests are invited to relax with a book, is filled with fine English and American antiques. Enjoy afternoon tea, lemonade and cookies in front of the fire. Guests are greeted in the morning with freshly brewed coffee and homemade muffins. Breakfasts are healthy and delicious with fresh fruits, pancakes, savory French toast, eggs and grits.

Staying at the inn is a unique experience. The guest rooms have been individually decorated, with fresh flowers and elegant furnishings. All the rooms have televisions, telephones, private baths and some have fireplaces.

Guests are encouraged to explore the landscaped gardens and relax by the fountain. Gourmet picnic lunches and suppers, available by request, are perfect for the beach. In the evening, guests enjoy hors d'oeuvres and a glass of wine or a cocktail on the wrap-around verandah. There is also a wonderful selection of homemade desserts, including chocolate cake and pecan pie.

Shrimp Gumbo

In a large saucepan, combine the bacon, ham, sausage, onion, red and green peppers and cook until onions are translucent. Sprinkle flour over meat and vegetable mixture until it gains a paste-like consistency. Cook for another 5 minutes.

In a stock pot, add the remaining ingredients and cook on medium-high heat until mixture begins to bubble. Lower heat and cook for another 10 to 15 minutes.

Serve hot with steamed white rice.

Serves 4
Preparation Time:
 30 Minutes

 8 oz. bacon, chopped
 8 oz. smoked ham, diced
 8 oz. smoked sausage, chopped
 1 medium onion, chopped
 ½ red pepper, chopped
 ½ green pepper, chopped
 ¼ cup flour, sifted
 1 can diced tomatoes, drained
 ½ lb. okra
 ¼ cup tomato paste
 2 qts. chicken stock
 Cayenne, white pepper and salt to taste
 Curry powder to taste
 Thyme, ground to taste
 Chili powder to taste
 Garlic, chopped to taste
 Cumin, ground to taste
 1 lb. shrimp, peeled, deveined
 2 cups white rice, cooked

RICHLAND STREET BED AND BREAKFAST

Richland Street Bed and Breakfast
1425 Richland Street
Columbia, South Carolina 29201
(803) 779-7001
ROOM RATES: $79–$120

The Richland Street Bed and Breakfast is a Victorian-style home in Columbia's Historic Preservation District. Located a short drive from museums, restaurants, city parks, antique shops, business and government centers and the nationally acclaimed Riverbanks Zoological Park, the inn tries to please both business travelers and vacationers.

Each of the seven guest rooms includes a private bath as well as room to relax and enjoy the peace and quiet. The McNair Suite and the West Room both feature king-sized beds and whirlpool baths.

Richland Street Bed & Breakfast–1992
Columbia, South Carolina

Apple-Raisin Coffee Cake

I n a mixing bowl, cream the shortening and sugar. Add the eggs and flavoring. Beat well.

Sift together dry ingredients. Add to the creamed mixture, alternating with the sour cream. Fold in the raisins and apples.

Spread in a greased pan. Top with the chopped nuts. Bake at 350° for 35 to 40 minutes.

Serves 10
Preparation Time:
  50 Minutes
Preheat oven to 350°

½ cup shortening
1 cup sugar
2 eggs, beaten
1 tsp. rum flavoring
2 cups plain flour
1 tsp. baking powder
1 tsp. baking soda
½ tsp. salt
1 tsp. cinnamon
¼ tsp. nutmeg
1 cup sour cream
½ cup raisins
2 cups apples, grated
½ cup nuts, chopped

TENNESSEE: The Volunteer State

Thousands of Tennesseans volunteered for service in the War of 1812, giving Tennessee its nickname. Deeply divided by the slavery issue, Tennessee, which seceded on June 8, 1861, ultimately sent soldiers to both the Union and Confederate armies. Next to Virginia, it was the most fought-over battleground during the Civil War. The names Shiloh, Stones River, Chickamauga and Chattanooga are nearly as famous as Gettysburg. After the war, Tennessee was the first Confederate state to re-enter the Union (1866).

Ever a land of divisions, the Ku Klux Klan appeared at the same time as modern reforms, such as women's suffrage. Then the yellow fever epidemic of 1878 took so many thousands of lives that Memphis' charter was revoked until 1891.

The 20th century brought the Tennessee Valley Authority, which developed a huge system of dams throughout the region. Improved flood control, cheap electricity, good navigational facilities and large man-made lakes added to the success of the state. Tourism exploded as visitors came to soak up the scenery of the Great Smoky Mountains, the glitter of the Grand Old Opry and the home of the Tennessee Walking Horse.

Tennessee is still divided culturally and geographically into two distinct regions: eastern and middle Tennessee, a series of high ridges, rolling hills and undulating valleys marking the highest points in the eastern United States and one of the oldest land massifs in the world; and western Tennessee, essentially flat land that drops off a sharp bluff onto the swampy bottomlands of the Mississippi River.

Tobacco is Tennessee's leading cash crop, and Tennessee leads the nation in the production of zinc, but the state is primarily industrial, rather than agricultural. Apparel, fabricated metal products and transportation equipment are the largest industries.

Famous Tennesseans include Roy Acuff, Davy Crockett, David Farragut, Alex Haley, William C. Handy, Sam Houston, Cordell Hull, Dolly Parton, Minnie Pearl and Dinah Shore.

Here are some of the highlights of a trip to Tennessee.

The Civil War battles of Lookout Mountain, Chickamauga and Missionary Ridge were fought near **CHATTANOOGA**. General William Tecumseh Sherman began his March to the Sea here. The LOOKOUT MOUNTAIN INCLINE RAILWAY, one of the steepest in the world (72.7 percent gradient), climbs to the summit, where you'll find ROCK CITY GARDENS, a city of natural rock formations. The 4,000-foot-long enchanted trail leads to Lovers' Leap and Observation Point, from which you can see seven states. Nearby is **CHICKAMAUGA AND CHATTANOOGA NATIONAL MILITARY PARK,** the oldest and largest national military park administered by the National Park Service.

GATLINBURG is an important handicraft area for the Southern Highlands. You can watch craftsmen demonstrating weaving, pottery, broom-making, woodworking and furniture manufacture. The SKY LIFT takes you from Main Street up the steep incline of 2,300-foot Crocket Mountain, where you'll enjoy panoramic scenic overlooks.

A blue, smokelike haze almost always shrouds the peaks of the **GREAT SMOKY MOUNTAINS NATIONAL PARK—** more than 520,000 acres evenly divided between North Carolina and Tennessee. Sixteen summits top 6,000 feet. The main ridge, which goes on for nearly forty miles, is more than 5,000 feet above sea level.

In 1873, former slaves founded the town of **HENNING.** Today this quiet town of late 19th century storefronts and Victorian houses only has a population of 800. Alex Haley grew up here, and here he learned about his ancestors and neighbors, who inspired Roots. You can visit the ALEX HALEY STATE HISTORIC SITE AND MUSEUM, where the writer lived from 1921 to 1929, and where he is now buried.

KNOXVILLE, host to the 1982 World's Fair, was once known as the Gateway to the West. It was the territorial capital from 1792–1796 and the state capital from 1796–1811 and again in 1817. The 400-acre UNIVERSITY OF TENNESSEE campus plays a vital role in the city's cultural life. The GOVERNOR WILLIAM BLOUNT MANSION (1792) and the KNOXVILLE MUSEUM OF ART are standout attractions in this city of 170,000.

Cook tent for the railroad in Monroe County, 1906

Photo: Tennessee State Library and Archives

MEMPHIS endured its near total destruction from yellow fever to become the largest city in Tennessee. At the beginning of the 20th century, on gaudy Beale Street, music legend W.C. Handy developed the "blues," and in 1977 Congress honored Memphis' musical heritage by declaring the city "The Home of the Blues." In the 1950s, Elvis Presley—The King—exploded onto the world scene from a Memphis recording studio. Another King—Martin Luther King—was tragically assassinated in Memphis in 1968. Today this capital of the Mississippi Delta is the dominant metropolitan area of west Tennessee, Mississippi and Arkansas. GRACELAND, Elvis Presley's 15,000-square-foot mansion, is generally mobbed. Stand in line for a 1½-hour tour of the pool room, TV room, music room, formal living and dining rooms, kitchen and den, all decorated as they were when The King lived here. The NATIONAL CIVIL RIGHTS MUSEUM, which contains interpretive exhibits and displays of key events in the civil rights movement, is housed in the Lorraine Motel, where Martin Luther King was assassinated.

Everything comes together in **NASHVILLE**. More Bibles are printed here than in almost any other U.S. city. There are 800 churches here, including the headquarters of the Southern Baptist Convention and the United Methodist Publishing House, which lead some to call Nashville "the Protestant Vatican" and others to call it "the buckle on the Bible Belt." It's also called "The Athens of the South," due to its Greek architecture, its devotion to the arts and to the perfect replica of THE PARTHENON, found in Centennial Park. Nashville is also the insurance and banking center for the entire region. But all this pales in comparison with Nashville's predominant $2.5 billion industry—Nashville is "Music City USA." It produces more than half of the singles records released in the country. And it is home to the GRAND OLE OPRY, the longest-running radio program in history, which started in 1925 as the WSM Barn Dance. Because the broadcast followed a segment of Grand Opera, announcer George Hay introduced his homespun country music program as, "The Grand Ole Opry" one night. And the name has stuck for nearly 75 years!

The COUNTRY MUSIC HALL OF FAME displays costumes, films, Elvis Presley's "solid gold" Cadillac and gold piano. It takes fully two days to see everything there is to see at OPRYLAND USA, an entertainment complex of world-class dimensions, which includes the GRAND OLE OPRY (try to be there Friday or Saturday for the 2½ hour show, broadcast from the 4,400-seat Grand Ole Opry House), the GENERAL JACKSON, a paddle wheel showboat; the 120-acre OPRYLAND THEME PARK, OPRYLAND USA RIVER TAXIS, the NASHVILLE NETWORK (TNN) and the COUNTRY MUSIC NETWORK (CMT). In

☆

between all the things to do, you might consider staying at the OPRYLAND HOTEL, which features more than 10,000 tropical plants in its conservatory. THE HERMITAGE, Andrew Jackson's 625-acre estate, contains much of the original furniture and fixtures, plus nearly all of the former president's personal effects.

THE MUSEUM OF APPALACHIA in Norris is a pioneer mountain village containing 35 authentic log structures, cabins, barns, blacksmith shop, cobbler's shop, a church, school and mule-powered molasses mill, as well as demonstrations of pioneer skills and musical performances.

A complete city was built at **OAK RIDGE** during World War II, which resulted in the first atomic bomb and the invention of the nuclear reactor. The AMERICAN MUSEUM OF SCIENCE AND ENERGY contains one of the world's largest energy exhibits.

PIGEON FORGE, adjacent to the Great Smoky Mountains,

Grocery hack

Photo: Tennessee State Library and Archives

is home to DOLLYWOOD, a 125-acre theme park owned and operated by Dolly Parton. Working craft shops, thrill rides, shows and the Dolly Parton Museum are only part of the fun. There are 150 big-name concerts during the season and more than 40 live performances every day. Allow a full day. You won't be disappointed.

Visit **SHELBYVILLE** and its 44 farms and stables to see the home of the Tennessee Walking Horse. Two thousand of these horses perform at the Tennessee Walking Horse National Celebration during late August each year.

More than 109,000 soldiers fought at **SHILOH NATIONAL MILITARY PARK** on April 6–7, 1862, and 24,000 were dead, missing or wounded when the smoke cleared from that bloodiest battle of the Civil War. After the battle, General Grant said, "I gave up all idea of saving the Union except by complete conquest."

★

212 MARKET

212 Market
NEW AMERICAN CUISINE
212 Market Street
Chattanooga, Tennessee
(423) 265-1212
Lunch Monday–Friday 11AM–3PM
Lunch Saturday 11:30AM–3PM
Dinner Monday–Saturday 5PM–9:30PM
AVERAGE DINNER FOR TWO: $55

L ocated near the Tennessee Aquarium, 212 Market certainly swims its own course when it comes to delicious and exciting cuisine. Thanks to its cutting-edge culinary approach, 212 Market has become a hot spot in Chattanooga. The chefs bring with them inventiveness and backgrounds that include French, South American and Californian, to name a few.

During the holiday season, Chef Susan Moses conjures up magical blown-sugar ornaments that can be used for desserts or special occasions. The ornaments are so lifelike that diners often do a double take. She has created everything from birds perched on wine glass rims and fruit basket centerpieces to mice on roller skates.

While the menu changes seasonally, past entrées have included Pesto Primavera Pasta, Spinach Walnut Ravioli, Maryland Crab Cakes with Roasted Red Bell Pepper Sauce, Greek Salad, BBQ Chicken Quesadilla and Pecan-Crusted Chicken Club Sandwiches.

212 MARKET'S MENU FOR SIX

Mushroom-Couscous Strudel

Mushroom-Couscous Strudel

I n a large stock pot combine the couscous with the vegetables. Add the boiling chicken stock. Cover and remove from the heat. Let stand for 10 minutes or until fluffy.

Add the lemon juice, parsley and basil to couscous. Refrigerate to chill.

Sauté the mushrooms with shallots and garlic in some olive oil over medium heat. Deglaze the pan with the white wine. When cooled, add to the chilled couscous.

Serve over baby greens tossed with dressing.

Serves 6
Preparation Time:
30 Minutes
(note refrigeration time)

6 cups couscous
1 cup celery, diced fine
1 cup red onion, diced fine
1 cup red bell pepper, diced fine
1 cup green bell pepper, diced fine
1 cup carrot, diced fine
1 gal. chicken stock, boiling
Juice from 1 lemon
½ cup parsley, chopped
¼ cup basil, chopped
5 mushrooms, sliced
½ cup shallots, chopped
½ cup garlic, chopped
Olive oil for sautéing
1½ cups white wine
1 lb. baby greens
Vinaigrette to taste

★

LA TOURELLE

La Tourelle
FRENCH CUISINE
2146 Melrose Avenue
Memphis, Tennessee
(901) 726-5771
Dinner 6PM–10PM
AVERAGE DINNER FOR TWO: $80

Named for its unique tower, La Tourelle has enticed Memphis diners with fabulous French cuisine since 1977. Proprietors Glenn and Martha Hays have succeeded in turning a beautiful Victorian house into a grand restaurant that feels like home. The quietly elegant atmosphere and the owners' commitment to excellence make La Tourelle a Tennessee favorite. Honored as the "Best Restaurant" in Memphis, it's the perfect place for an intimate dinner for two or a celebration in any one of the various dining rooms.

Award-winning Executive Chef Lynn Kennedy-Tilyou's inventive menu mixes French and Mediterranean cuisines. Some of the tasty delights are Roasted Salmon with Curried Dijon Sauce and Winter Oranges, Marinated Portobellos with Avocado, Celeriac Salad and Red Pepper Coulis and Seared Foie Gras with Champagne Pear Sauce.

LA TOURELLE'S MENU FOR SIX

Greens with Tarragon Dressing and Seasoned Almonds

Blue Cheese-Crusted Mahi Mahi

Banana Walnut Fritters

Greens with Tarragon Dressing and Seasoned Almonds

F or the almonds, combine the chili powder, sugar and salt in a large mixing bowl.

Whisk the egg white until frothy. Add some of the egg white to the almonds and stir. The almonds should be sticky from the egg white, not wet. You will not use the whole egg white.

Toss the sticky almonds into the chili powder-sugar mixture and toss well to coat. Place on parchment-lined sheet pan and bake until golden brown. Stir almonds lightly to break up. Do not overstir. Let cool.

Peel and break the orange into segments.

Peel and seed the cucumber; cut into thin, half-moon slices.

Cut the apple into slices.

For the dressing, place the egg yolk, lemon juice and zest, vinegar, honey and mustard in a bowl and stir well. Stir in the salad oil in a slow, steady stream. Add the tarragon and season with salt and pepper. If the dressing is too thick, add cold water to thin. This dressing is best made several hours ahead of time.

Toss the mixed lettuces with the oranges, cucumbers and tarragon dressing.

Serve the salad topped with sliced apples and seasoned almonds.

Serves 6
Preparation Time:
  20 Minutes
(note cooling time)
Preheat oven to 350°

  1 Tbsp. chili powder
  ¾ cup sugar
  1 egg white, slightly beaten
    Salt to taste
  ½ cup almonds, blanched, sliced
  3 oranges
  1 cucumber
  1 Granny Smith apple
  1 egg yolk
  ⅓ lemon, juiced, zested
  2 tsps. raspberry vinegar
  2 tsps. honey
1¾ Tbsps. Dijon mustard
1¾ cups salad oil
1½ Tbsps. tarragon, chopped
    Pepper to taste
  9 cups assorted lettuce, washed

Blue Cheese-Crusted Mahi Mahi

Serves 6
Preparation Time:
  20 Minutes
Preheat oven to 450°

  ½ **cup bread crumbs**
1¾ **tsps. Worcestershire**
     sauce
  1 **tsp. lemon juice**
1½ **Tbsps. butter, clarified**
2¾ **lbs. mahi mahi fillets**
  ½ **lb. blue cheese,**
     crumbled
     Juice from 1 lemon
  1 **tsp. pepper**

Combine the bread crumbs, Worcestershire sauce, lemon juice and butter and mix well.

Portion the boned mahi mahi into 6 oz. fillets. Place mahi mahi on a slightly greased sheet pan and top each fillet with lemon juice, pepper and 3 Tbsps. of the bread-crumb mixture. Top with 2 Tbsps. blue cheese.

Bake in a 450° oven for 10 to 15 minutes. The fish should be cooked, the blue cheese should be bubbling and the bread crumbs should be golden brown in color.

Banana Walnut Fritters

Melt the chocolate in top of a double boiler with the water temperature at 120°.

In a separate saucepan, bring the heavy cream to a boil. Stir into the melted chocolate. Stir in the Grand Marnier. Remove from heat. Keep warm until serving.

In a mixing bowl, combine the egg and sugar and whip lightly.

Blanch the orange and lemon zest lightly in a small pot of water. Drain and chop fine. Add the citrus juices, salt and chopped zest to the egg-sugar mixture.

In a separate pan, combine the white wine, flour and baking powder and bring the mixture to a boil. Stir into the egg-juice mixture. Blend until smooth. Add the chopped nuts and banana to the batter.

In a frying pan, heat the oil to 350°.

Drop batter from a spoon into hot oil and fry until golden brown. Drain on paper towels.

Serve with whipped cream and chocolate sauce.

Serves 6
Preparation Time:
  30 Minutes

4 oz. chocolate
1 cup heavy cream
1 Tbsp. Grand Marnier
1 egg
1 Tbsp. sugar
  Juice and zest from
  1 orange
  Juice and zest from
  1 lemon
  Salt to taste
1 oz. white wine
½ cup flour
1 tsp. baking powder
½ cup walnuts, chopped
1 banana
  Oil for frying
  Whipped cream,
  garnish

SOUTHSIDE GRILL

Southside Grill
SOUTHERN CUISINE
1400 Coward Street
Chattanooga, Tennessee
(423) 266-9211
Lunch Monday–Friday 11AM–5:30PM
Lunch Saturday Noon–5:30PM
Dinner 5:30 PM Daily
AVERAGE DINNER FOR TWO: $70

Diners often refer to Southside Grill as one of the best restaurants in the South and it's easy to see why. No matter how bizarre the request, Executive Chef Nathan Winowich meets it in a way that makes both the customer and the kitchen happy.

Chef Nathan is self-taught and keenly aware of the importance of mentoring new talent by welcoming apprentices from the American Culinary Federation.

Menu highlights include Pasta with Pulled Chicken, Homemade Roasted Fennel Sausage, Oven-Dried Tomatoes and Rich Mushroom Broth, Thin-Sliced Portobello and Rare Charred Beef Tenderloin with Mixed Greens and Roasted Garlic Emulsion, Pan-Fried Trout Cake with Spinach and Bacon, Dried Red Potatoes and Smoked Trout Rémoulade and Blood Orange Sorbet with Lemon Cinnamon Curd and Pistachio Shortbread.

SOUTHSIDE GRILL'S MENU FOR FOUR

Apple-Smoked Bacon-Wrapped Quail Breasts with Sage Risotto Cakes and

Warm Mustard Pecan Vinaigrette

Roasted Sweet Potato Purée

Fried Green Tomatoes with Creamy Lobster Succotash

Apple-Smoked Bacon-Wrapped Quail Breasts with Sage Risotto Cakes and Warm Mustard Pecan Vinaigrette

Marinate the quail in a bowl with maple syrup, mustard, pepper and ½ cup olive oil. Refrigerate overnight.

To make the vinaigrette: Place the red onions, pecans, mustard seeds, balsamic vinegar and Dijon mustard in a bowl and slowly whisk in 1 cup of olive oil. Let sit in a warm place for 15 minutes or until slightly warm to the touch.

To make the risotto: In a medium sauté pan, sauté the onion in butter until translucent. Add rice and cook until slightly browned, while stirring constantly. Then slowly add ½ cup of chicken stock, then 4 Tbsps. of chicken stock every 2 to 3 minutes until completely absorbed. Rice should be creamy and al dente. Remove from heat and stir in sage. Spread in a flat pan and allow to cool.

Once cooled, mix the risotto in a bowl with eggs and bread crumbs, then form into eight 2 oz. balls slightly flattening each, then set aside. Place sliced bacon flat on a cutting board, then tightly wrap each piece of quail in a slice of bacon. Refrigerate for 1 hour before cooking. Grill quail breasts carefully until bacon begins to brown, then place them in a 350° oven for 8 minutes.

If grill is not available, pan-sear in a non-stick pan and finish in oven. Heat the peanut oil and while quail is in the oven, fry the risotto cakes until golden brown (2 per person).

To serve, place 1 risotto cake in the middle of each plate and gently lean 3 cooked quail breasts around it. Place the second risotto cake on top and finish by drizzling vinaigrette over the quail and risotto cakes.

Garnish with a fresh vegetable of your choice.

Serves 4
Preparation Time:
  1 Hour
(note marinating time)

- 12 boneless quail breasts
- ¼ cup maple syrup
- ¼ cup whole-grain mustard
- 1 Tbsp. black pepper
- 1½ cups olive oil
- ½ cup red onion, diced
- ¾ cup pecans, toasted, chopped
- 1 Tbsp. mustard seeds, toasted
- ½ cup balsamic vinegar
- 2 Tbsps. Dijon mustard
- 1 medium onion, diced
- 1 stick butter
- 1½ cups arborio rice
- 1½ cups chicken stock or broth
- 15 sage leaves, chopped
- 2 eggs
- ½ cup bread crumbs
- 12 slices apple-smoked bacon
- 3 cups peanut oil
  Salt and pepper to taste

☆

Roasted Sweet Potato Purée

Serves 4 to 6
Preparation Time:
  40 Minutes
Preheat oven to 350°

  3 **large sweet potatoes,**
    peeled, halved
    Salt and pepper to
    taste
½ **tsp. nutmeg**
½ **tsp. cinnamon**
  5 **Tbsps. brown sugar**
  8 **Tbsps. olive oil**
  2 **stalks celery, chopped**
  1 **medium carrot,**
    chopped
  1 **medium onion,**
    chopped
  8 **cups of chicken broth**
  2 **cups sour cream**

P lace the sweet potatoes in a roasting pan and sprinkle with salt, pepper, nutmeg, cinnamon and brown sugar, then drizzle with half the olive oil and roast at 350° until fork-tender.

In a large saucepan, sauté the celery, carrot and onion in 4 Tbsps. of olive oil for 10 minutes. Add the chicken broth and cook on medium high heat. Remove the roasted sweet potatoes from oven and chop roughly. Then put them in the saucepan with the broth and boil for 20 minutes.

Reduce heat and add sour cream, then carefully pour into a blender or food processor and purée until smooth. This may take 2 to 3 batches, depending on the size of the blender. Season to taste.

☆

Fried Green Tomatoes with Creamy Lobster Succotash

I n a large mixing bowl, season the flour with salt and pepper. Set aside.

In a separate bowl, whisk the eggs and milk together and set aside.

In another bowl, combine the bread crumbs and Parmesan cheese.

Dust the tomato slices in the flour mixture, then dip them into the egg mixture, then generously coat them with bread crumb mixture. After that, dip back into egg mixture and once again into the bread crumb mixture. Set aside.

In a large frying pan, heat the peanut oil. Deep fry tomato slices until they are golden brown and tender. Remove from oil, being careful not to break them, and set aside on absorbent paper towels to drain.

Sauté the corn, scallions, bell peppers and lima beans on medium heat in a 10-inch sauté pan with in 2 Tbsps. of olive oil for 4 minutes, then add the lobster and continue cooking for 1 minute more. Add the cream, garlic and spice blend and let mixture reduce for 3 minutes. Season to taste.

To serve, place 1 tomato slice on each plate and pour ¼ of the succotash over it. Top with another tomato, then garnish with chopped chives if desired.

Serves 4
Preparation Time:
  25 Minutes

- 2 cups all-purpose flour
- 2 Tbsps. salt
- 1 Tbsp. pepper
- 2 eggs
- 1 cup milk
- 1 lb. bread crumbs
- ½ cup Parmesan cheese, freshly grated
- 2 green tomatoes, sliced ¾-inch thick (roughly 8 slices)
- 3 cups peanut oil
- 2 ears yellow corn, steamed, cut from cob
- 1 bunch scallions, chopped
- 1 red bell pepper, diced
- 1 green bell pepper, diced
- 1 cup lima beans, cooked
- 2 Tbsps. olive oil
- ¾ cup lobster meat, steamed, chopped
- 1 cup cream
- 1 garlic clove, chopped
- 1 tsp. Cajun spice blend
  Chives, chopped, garnish (optional)

★

BUCKHORN INN

Buckhorn Inn
2140 Tudor Mountain Road
Gatlinburg, Tennessee 37738
(423) 436-4668
ROOM RATES: $105–$160

Upon entering the Buckhorn Inn, guests find themselves in a long, spacious room with a stone fireplace, grand piano, book-lined walls and large windows facing the ever-changing panorama of the Great Smoky Mountains. Guests may also enjoy the mountain view from the covered flagstone terrace.

Upstairs five comfortable, intimate rooms are beautifully furnished with antiques, artwork and private baths. In addition, four private guest cottages are nestled nearby in the woodlands. The inn is surrounded by 35 acres of forest, groomed meadows, terraced flower garden, quiet walkways and a pond with ducks and fish.

The Buckhorn Inn employs two professional chefs who prepare sumptuous breakfasts and four-course gourmet dinners.

The inn is in the midst of the "Great Smoky Arts and Crafts Community," the largest concentration of independent artists and craftspeople in the world. The locale offers convenient access to hiking and sightseeing in the national park, as well as horseback riding, golf and shopping.

Italian Cracked Wheat Bread

Combine the warm water, yeast and honey. Let sit until bubbly, about 10 minutes.

Add 1 cup cool water, whole wheat flour and bread flour. Mix until smooth. Loosely cover with plastic and let sit for 4 to 8 hours. The mixture may have to be punched down.

Pour the boiling water over the cracked wheat. Let sit for at least 30 minutes.

Add cracked wheat, salt and enough all-purpose flour to make a sticky dough that still barely holds its shape.

Turn onto a floured surface and knead. Add all-purpose flour to keep it from sticking, kneading until the dough becomes elastic. Cover and let rest for 30 minutes.

Form into desired shape and place on greased baking sheet. Let rise to double in size. Make diagonal slashes on top.

In a separate bowl, mix the egg and 1 Tbsp. water. Brush the egg-water mixture on top of the loaf. Bake for 10 minutes at 450°. Lower heat to 400° and bake for an additional 20 minutes or until golden brown.

Yield:
  1 loaf
Preparation Time:
  45 minutes
(note rising time)
Preheat oven to 350°

  1 cup warm water
  1 tsp. yeast
  1 tsp. honey
  1 cup + 1 Tbsp. cool
    water
  1 cup whole wheat flour
1½ cups bread flour
  ¾ cup boiling water
  ¼ cup cracked wheat
  1 Tbsp. salt
  2 cups all-purpose flour
  1 egg

LOEWS VANDERBILT PLAZA HOTEL

Loews Vanderbilt Plaza Hotel
2100 West End Avenue
Nashville, Tennessee 37203
(615) 320-1700
(800) 23 LOEWS
ROOM RATES: $154–$184

L oews Vanderbilt Plaza Hotel displays sweeping views of Nashville, the Cumberland River and the Tennessee hills beyond. Yet it is in the very heart of the city's educational, medical and business district and adjacent to renowned Vanderbilt University.

Inside the hotel, quiet elegance prevails, with a stately travertine lobby with faux marble colonnades, Aubusson tapestries and original fine art. If pampering is a must for you, the ultimate is one of the hotel's 12 suites, offering a private French balcony and fireplace or wet bar.

Loews Vanderbilt Plaza Hotel features three tempting places to dine. The Plaza Grill is known for its light and simple fare, while Sfuzzi serves up fine Italian cuisine in a stylish, faux-Romanesque-ruins decor. Relaxing to live entertainment in the Garden Lounge is another option.

Crab Cakes

n a mixing bowl, combine the crab meat, crawfish tails, seasoning, lime juice, mayonnaise, egg, bread crumbs, parsley and Worcestershire sauce.

Form into 4 oz. cakes.

Sauté crab cakes in a hot, oiled sauté pan until golden brown.

Serve immediately.

Yield:
  7 cakes, 4 oz. each
Preparation Time:
  15 Minutes

1 lb. crab meat, picked
   clean of shells
½ lb. crawfish tails
1 tsp. Old Bay Seasoning
1 tsp. lime juice
½ cup mayonnaise
1 egg, beaten
½ cup bread crumbs
2 Tbsps. parsley,
   chopped
2 dashes Worcestershire
   sauce
2 Tbsps. oil

★

LYRIC SPRINGS COUNTRY INN

Lyric Springs Country Inn
7306 South Harpeth Road
Franklin, Tennessee 37064
(800) 621-7824
(615) 329-3385
ROOM RATES: $135

L yric Springs Country Inn is nestled in historic and picturesque Williamson County on the banks of South Harpeth Creek. The area has been famous for Southern hospitality since right after the Civil War and this country inn continues the Southern traditions.

The bed and breakfast is home to songwriter and Nashville insider Patsy Bruce. Music and history abound in Mama's Cowboy Saloon and in the guest rooms, which bear such names as Waltz Suite, Bluegrass Suite and Melody Suite.

Each room is a gallery of 1940s textiles, romantic quilt-covered tables and chairs, dainty handkerchiefs and spectacular needlework displayed as art. Throughout the inn, there is an assortment of antique wrought iron, McCoy vases and all sorts of fancy and plain "old things," displayed in a variety of unique ways.

Gourmet food is the owner's hobby. Meals are served in a beautiful garden room overlooking the lake, by the creek or around the fountain in the antique brick courtyard.

Gumbo Ya Ya

Season chicken with salt, cayenne pepper and garlic. Measure flour into a large paper bag. Add the chicken pieces and shake until well coated. Remove the chicken and reserve the extra flour.

In a large skillet, brown the chicken in very hot oil; remove chicken and set aside. Stir oil that remains in skillet with a wire whisk to loosen all the browned flour from the bottom and sides of pan.

Whisk in 1 cup of the reserved flour and stir constantly until the mixture of oil and flour (the roux) becomes dark brown. Remove from heat and add the onions, celery and bell peppers, stirring constantly so they do not burn. Transfer roux and vegetables to a large, heavy saucepan.

Add the chicken stock to the roux and vegetables and bring to a boil, stirring. Lower the heat to a simmer and add the garlic, sausage and chicken. Continue cooking until the chicken is tender, about 1¾ to 2 hours.

Adjust the seasonings to taste and serve in gumbo bowls over steamed rice.

Serves 8
Preparation Time:
  2½ Hours

  1 **large roasting chicken, about 5 lbs., disjointed and cut into 10 pieces**
    Salt to taste
    Cayenne pepper to taste
    Powdered garlic to taste
2½ **cups flour**
  1 **cup vegetable oil**
  2 **cups onion, coarsely chopped**
1½ **cups celery, coarsely chopped**
  2 **cups green bell pepper, coarsely chopped**
  6 **cups chicken stock**
1½ **tsps. fresh garlic, minced**
  1 **lb. andouille sausage, finely diced**
  4 **cups cooked rice**

☆

Fabulous Fudge Cake

Serves 8
Preparation Time:
   45 Minutes
Preheat oven to 375°

   3 squares unsweetened
      chocolate
2¼ cups cake flour, sifted
   2 tsps. baking soda
   ½ tsp. salt
   ½ cup butter or
      margarine
2¼ cups firmly packed
      brown sugar
   3 eggs
   2 tsps. vanilla
   ½ cup buttermilk
   1 cup boiling water
      Frosting (recipe
      follows)

G rease bottoms of three 9 × 1½-inch layer cake pans; line pans with waxed paper and grease the paper.

Melt the chocolate in a small saucepan over very low heat. Set aside.

Sift together the cake flour, baking soda and salt onto waxed paper.

Cream the butter or margarine in a large bowl with a spoon or electric mixer at medium speed. Gradually add the sugar and beat until the mixture is fluffy.

Beat in eggs, 1 at a time, until thick. Stir in the vanilla and chocolate with a spoon or mixer at low speed.

Add the sifted dry ingredients, a third at a time, alternating with buttermilk, stirring by hand or with mixer at low speed, just until blended. Stir in the boiling water. Pour into cake pans.

Bake in a 375° oven for 25 to 30 minutes, or until the centers spring back when lightly pressed with fingertip.

Cool in the pans on wire racks for 5 minutes. Loosen around the edges with a knife, turn out onto racks, remove the waxed paper and let cool completely.

Put the layers together and frost.

☆

Chocolate Frosting

Combine the sugar, cornstarch and salt in a medium-sized saucepan. Stir in boiling water until well blended. Cook, stirring constantly, until the mixture thickens. Add the chocolate squares and butter or margarine. Continue cooking and stirring until the chocolate and butter melt. Remove from heat and stir in vanilla.

Pour into a medium-sized bowl.

Chill, stirring several times, until thick enough to spread.

Preparation Time:
45 Minutes

1½ cups sugar
6 Tbsps. cornstarch
¼ tsp. salt
1½ cups boiling water
3 squares unsweetened chocolate
¼ cup butter or margarine
1 tsp. vanilla

☆

OPRYLAND HOTEL

Opryland Hotel
2800 Opryland Drive
Nashville, Tennessee 37214-1297
(615) 889-1000
ROOM RATES: $209–$920

I magine dining, listening to a world-renowned pianist and watching a glittering light-and-water show while a 40-foot waterfall rumbles in the background—all under a two-and-a-half-acre skylight. Simply put: There's no place else quite like the Opryland Hotel. It is a panorama of tastes and styles.

The hotel has 1,891 rooms, including 120 suites and more than 500 Garden Terrace rooms, overlooking the tropical Cascades or the breathtaking Conservatory, a two-acre Victorian garden under glass.

There is always something for guests to do at the Opryland Hotel. Some guests enjoy visiting the nearby historical sites. Of course there's the Opryland Theme Park, with thrilling rides and dazzling live musicals, including pure country, bluegrass and Broadway and Hollywood award-winners.

Guests may also enjoy cruises by sunlight or moonlight, taking a swim or playing a round of golf on the 18-hole championship golf course.

Southern Velvet Soup

Tie the bay leaves, parsley, black peppercorns, white peppercorns and thyme in a cheesecloth bag to make a bouquet garni.

Melt ½ cup butter in a stock pot. Add the bouquet garni, celery, onions and oysters. Sauté until the celery and onions are tender.

Add the brandy, stirring to deglaze the stock pot.

Add the clam juice and fish stock.

Cook over medium heat for 45 minutes to 1 hour or until the oysters are cooked through. Remove the bouquet garni.

Return the oysters, celery, onions and soup stock to the stock pot. Stir in the cream. Cook until heated through.

Melt the remaining butter in a saucepan or skillet. Add the flour. Cook until the flour is browned, stirring constantly.

Add to the soup and mix well. Season with salt and pepper. Stir in the sherry just before serving.

Serves 8
Preparation Time:
  1¼ **Hours**

  2 **bay leaves**
  ¼ **bunch parsley, coarsely**
     chopped
  2 **tsps. black**
     peppercorns
  2 **tsps. white**
     peppercorns
  3 **fresh thyme sprigs**
  ½ **cup butter**
  4 **cups celery, chopped**
  2 **cups onions, chopped**
  1 **qt. oysters**
  ¼ **cup brandy**
  1 **cup clam juice**
  2¼ **cups fish stock**
  2 **cups cream**
  ½ **cup butter**
  1½ **cups flour**
     Salt and pepper to
     taste
  ½ **cup sherry**

☆

UNION STATION HOTEL

Union Station Hotel
1001 Broadway
Nashville, Tennessee 37203
(800) 331-2123
(615) 726-1001
ROOM RATES: $95–$125

Built at the height of Nashville's social and economic growth, the Union Station Hotel is a landmark in the heart of Music City and is listed on the National Register of Historic Places.

Originally opened in 1900 as a train station, guests are greeted in a modern lobby with a stained-glass skylight, silvered mirrors, bas-relief artwork with gold trim and a black marble fountain. The barrel-vaulted ceiling has original stained-glass panels. A classic example of Romanesque-Revival architecture, the hotel is a limestone building with a massive clock tower and guest rooms with 22-foot-high ceilings.

Over the past 16 years, Arthur's Restaurant has been serving up award-winning meals to Nashvillians, as well as celebrities, journalists, government dignitaries and business leaders from around the nation and the world. The restaurant features an eclectic menu with recipes from North America, Europe, Africa and Asia.

Roasted Trout with Pancetta and Olive Tapenade

F or the tapenade, place the olives, capers, lemon juice and thyme in a food processor. Process to a coarse purée. Set aside.

Slice open each trout and put ½ Tbsp. of the tapenade inside. Wrap each trout loosely with 2 strips of pancetta. Brush with olive oil and place in an oiled roasting pan.

Roast for 10 to 12 minutes at 400°.

Cooking Secret: This dish is delicious over roasted baby vegetables.

Serves 4
Preparation Time:
  20 Minutes
Preheat oven to 400°

1 cup Niçoise or
  Kalamata olives, pitted
¼ cup capers
  Juice from 1 lemon
1 tsp. lemon thyme,
  chopped
4 trout, dressed,
  boneless, headless,
  8 oz. each
8 pancetta strips, thinly
  sliced, 8 inches long
2 Tbsps. olive oil
4 lemon wedges

☆

Index

About the Author

KATHLEEN DEVANNA FISH, author of the popular "Secrets" series, is a gourmet cook and gardener who is always on the lookout for recipes with style and character.

In addition to *Cooking Secret's From America's South*, Kathleen has written the award-winning *Great Vegetarian Cookbook, Pacific Northwest Cooking Secrets, Cooking Secrets for Healthy Living, The Gardener's Cookbook, The Great California Cookbook, California Wine Country Cooking Secrets, San Francisco's Cooking Secrets, Monterey's Cooking Secrets, New England's Cooking Secrets, Cape Cod's Cooking Secrets* and *Cooking and Traveling Inn Style*.

Before embarking on a writing and publishing career, she owned and operated three businesses in the travel and hospitality industry.

ROBERT FISH, award-winning photojournalist, produces the images that bring together the concept of the "Secrets" series.

In addition to taking the cover photographs, Robert explores the food and wine of each region, helping to develop the overview upon which each book is based.

Bon Vivant Press

A division of The Millennium Publishing Group

PO Box 1994 • Monterey, CA 93942

800-524-6826 • 408-373-0592 • FAX 408-373-3567 • http://www.millpub.com

Send _____ copies of *Cooking with the Masters of Food & Wine* at $34.95 each.

Send _____ copies of *The Elegant Martini* at $17.95 each.

Send _____ copies of *Cooking Secrets from Around the World* at $15.95 each.

Send _____ copies of *Cooking Secrets from America's South* at $15.95 each.

Send _____ copies of *Louisiana Cooking Secrets* at $15.95 each.

Send _____ copies of *Pacific Northwest Cooking Secrets* at $15.95 each.

Send _____ copies of *Cooking Secrets for Healthy Living* at $15.95 each.

Send _____ copies of *The Great California Cookbook* at $15.95 each.

Send _____ copies of *The Gardener's Cookbook* at $15.95 each.

Send _____ copies of *The Great Vegetarian Cookbook* at $15.95 each.

Send _____ copies of *California Wine Country Cooking Secrets* at $14.95 each.

Send _____ copies of *San Francisco's Cooking Secrets* at $13.95 each.

Send _____ copies of *Monterey's Cooking Secrets* at $13.95 each.

Send _____ copies of *New England's Cooking Secrets* at $14.95 each.

Send _____ copies of *Cape Cod's Cooking Secrets* at $14.95 each.

Send _____ copies of *Jewish Cooking Secrets From Here and Far* at $14.95 each.

Send _____ copies of *Pets Welcome California* at $15.95 each.

Send _____ copies of *Pets Welcome America's South* at $15.95 each.

Add $3.00 postage and handling for the first book ordered and $1.50 for each additional book.
Please add $1.08 sales tax per book, for those books shipped to California addresses.

Please charge my ☐ Visa ☐ MasterCard   #_____

Expiration date_____Signature _____

Enclosed is my check for _____

Name _____

Address _____

City_____State_____Zip _____

☐ This is a gift. Send directly to:

Name _____

Address _____

City_____State_____Zip _____

☐ Autographed by the author
   Autographed to _____

NOTES